SuperCouples

Happy Reading!!

loads of wishes

Prachi Garg ~~

SuperCouples

Inspiring Stories of Couple-preneurs

Prachi Garg

Srishti
PUBLISHERS & DISTRIBUTORS

SRISHTI PUBLISHERS & DISTRIBUTORS
Registered Office: N-16, C.R. Park
New Delhi – 110 019
Corporate Office: 212A, Peacock Lane
Shahpur Jat, New Delhi – 110 049
editorial@srishtipublishers.com

First published by
Srishti Publishers & Distributors in 2017

Disclaimer: This is a work of non-fiction, charting the stories of nineteen couple-entrepreneurs and their startups. All the stories and pictures herein have been narrated and given to the author by the persons concerned and have been reproduced herein with their due permission. Although the author and publisher have made every effort to ensure that the information in this book was correct at press time, the author and publisher do not assume and hereby disclaim any liability to any party for any loss, damage, or disruption caused by errors or omissions, whether such errors or omissions result from negligence, accident, or any other cause.

Dedicated to
my father Brejesh Garg,
and mother Neeru Garg.

Contents

Acknowledgements

This book has been possible due to the enormous love and support that people have given to me. It was their constant support that kept me going and ensured that I should be able to deliver it on time. I would like to thank everyone for making the journey smooth for me.

Family members play a great role to make such accomplishments possible. In my case as well, this holds true. Each of them has been instrumental and has been there when required.

Mr. Arup Bose from Srishti Publishers for his faith in my concept and agreeing to publish the same.

Stuti Sharma, my editor, who undertook the tedious task of going through my manuscript, editing it and coming out with exciting ideas.

All my friends who provided me with constant moral support to make this happen.

All the readers of *Superwomen*, whose love inspired me to pen down *SuperCouples*.

And finally, all the lovely couples who took out time and shared their brilliant stories with me, so that I could share them with you all.

I hope all of you get inspired with their journeys and contribute to the progress of the nation.

A note from the author

Running a successful business with your soulmate has always been idyllic and intriguing for me. I always used to wonder how couples strike a balance between their personal and professional lives, especially when they are together all the time. In fact, working together helps determine your mutual career destinies, instead of spending many hours apart, working for someone else. This inspired me to speak to these wonderful couples across India, who planned to be partners in crime in everything, and decided to build a meaningful life together by co-creating something that brings them joy and fulfillment. However, this interaction about their journeys brought some key takeaways for me.

Be on the same page.

Keen alignment and shared vision are the keys to success for any business. Though couples share a level of intimacy and friendship, it is important that they are aligned on their career vision and their life goals too. Because only then will both of them be able to do justice with the enterprise.

Define your roles and responsibilities.

Since with couple-preneurs, the line between personal and business gets very blurred, it is very important to define their roles and responsibilities. In most of the interactions, I realised that division of roles had a great impact in making their partnership a successful one. If one of them is managing operations, then the better half would manage marketing. This not only avoids day to day conflicts, but also empowers both of their decision-making power. This has brought out the best in them, and also saved them from stepping into the other's shoes.

Maintain work-life (and love) balance.

It is very important to keep a check on how your business decisions are impacting your personal life. Either it can do wonders, or wreck everything. I came across many such examples during these interactions. So my two cents here would be to keep experimenting to see what works well for you as a couple, and how a decision can reinforce your love for each other.

Be kind, understanding and respectful.

It is very important to make sure that both of you respect each other. Since here lives are way too inter-wined, conflicts are bound to happen. It is important to handle them respectfully and keeping each other's priorities in mind.

For me, it is more like being married to your work, and at the same time getting the chance to spend quality time with your spouse. And I am sure most of the couple-preneurs I interacted with would agree to this. Most of them have been able to explore the other side of their spouse, which would not have been possible in the absence of this plunge. Their journey is definitely different, but as they always say: "No risk, no gain".

Happy reading and get inspired. :-)

Couple-preneurship: Balancing the act of business & love.
The journey of SuperCouples begins...

© Dheeraj Mrig

Meenakshi & Jey *founded* **Artologue: Art for all** *to keep their passion for art going, but have gone on to inspire people to see art in everything around them. They travel across the country to paint their messages of love, peace and elevation of humanity.*

Colours of Life – ARTOLOGUE

By Meenakshi & Jey

In this fast-paced life, we can still find people who dedicate themselves to their passion. These are the kind of people who dare to dream, and more importantly, dare to follow those dreams, no matter what. Such extraordinary men and women create magic wherever they go, in whatever they do. When you are around them, you can feel their energy, their creativity, and the beauty in their spirit that is both inspiring and humbling, all at once. When such people come together, one can expect nothing short of a spectacle. This might not necessarily be the blinding, glamorous, on-your-television kind of spectacle, but one that elevates its beholders in big ways and small. They enrich you and make you want to become a part of it. Such is the story of two artists, travellers and partners, and fundamentally, two fantastic humans who have been creating their own share of magic together.

Meenakshi had always been an admirer of art. Her liberating education and daring passion pushed her into being involved with various forms of art, and eventually made her into a learned connoisseur. Jey, on the other hand, is a writer and committed traveller who has a hunger for art and its appreciation. When the two met as family friends, their common interests brought them closer. From a cordial friendship between a school girl and a boy pursuing his Master's degree way back in 2001, this relationship evolved through years, growing in mutual admiration. With growing affection between them, coupled with common interests, this equation flowered into unsaid love. Eventually, with a ripened understanding and trust in each other, they tied the knot in 2010.

Apart from having common interests, Meenakshi and Jey had also participated in organizing several group and solo exhibitions. Understanding each other's interests, style and strengths is another aspect that encouraged them to explore different dimensions of life. Jey, in all these years, has continued his love for writing as a journalist, while Meenakshi has continued her pursuit of different forms of art. From afar, it would seem they're a a couple that leads an ordinary life and cultivates art as a form of a parallel hobby. But anyone who knows them well would know that they live a life many would not be able to comprehend. With an unusual modus operandi, Meenakshi and Jey have two unique members in their family – Hari Bhari and Kesariya – their companions-in-arms, quite literally. Amalgamating their love for art and travel, this couple has changed their style of vacations and made it into a movement – colouring different parts of the country.

"We used to travel to new places for vacations every year. We would also dedicate our time to painting over the weekends. So we thought why not combine these two ideas together!" recalls Jey. The idea started with the concept of bringing the joy of art to the common people.

"I find it ridiculous when people say that for art to be understood or adopted, you need a special taste, education or even acumen. I think everyone can be an artist; rather everyone is an artist – whether he or she is a cook, a teacher, a carpenter or even a doctor," Meenakshi explains candidly. With this basic motivation, the duo set out to spread art in the lives of people. With this motto at heart, they formulated their own concoction called Artologue – a story of art and travel.

What has art got to do with travelling, one might wonder. A simple explanation is that art is present wherever one goes – in the distant villages, in valleys, schools, houses by the shore or even in the doodles of dark alleys. Very often, they can be used to depict stories, to create harmony, to bring people together, or simply to beautify a space, creating a special ambience. That is exactly what Meenakshi and Jey endeavour to achieve. Spreading love, joy and colours everywhere they go, this couple steals time between Jey's job and Meenakshi's plans, catering to different kinds of audience across the country.

"This started as an experiment with some of our friends in Mumbai and Goa. The initial response was very encouraging and supportive, marking what later became a well-received journey of us as 'artwalle' (people of art)," Meenakshi speaks in retrospection. With over a hundred and twenty-five days of travel in the last four years, the couple has set an example of a different kind of travelling experience. Having spent less than a lakh rupees in the process, they have gone to different cities, towns and even villages across geographies, painting their messages of love, peace and the elevation of humanity.

"We are often invited by people to come and paint a message for them; sometimes they give us an idea of what they would like, while at other times, they just leave it up to us to engage them. It always turns into a beautiful experience in the end." Jey smiles knowingly.

Painting murals for friends and strangers, the twosome have earned many friends and well-wishers through their journey.

There are many stories that the two can narrate that begin with strangers and end with friendships made for life. The two are known to form exemplary connections with people of all ages and backgrounds.

So is this their profession or their hobby? Meenakshi laughs mischievously at this question and teases with questions asking what the definitions of a profession or a hobby are. Taking things on a serious note, Jey explains how Artologue really functions. Generally, the duo is invited over by individuals or organizations. Depending on the nature of the hosts and the scale of work, and as per their desire, the couple leaves it up to the people to pay them. This way, the liberty and authority of work still lies with Artologue, at the same time, not making it a burden for both ends to accomplish the project.

"There are times when people sponsor our travel, provide accommodation and hospitality, and open their doors and hearts for us. That counts for a lot of value, especially in sync with everything that Jey and I have set out to accomplish through the language of art," Meenakshi speaks emotionally, "That alone is more than what a pay cheque can buy."

But if you thought everything is smooth in this fantastic little fairy tale, you will only have known the happy end. Challenges come in all shapes and sizes for these artwalle too!

"We are under no illusion about the struggles that Artologue will have to pass through with each journey," Jey clarifies.

You have to admit that however beautiful the ideas, if they are unusual, they find it difficult to be accepted in a country like ours. The story is no different for Meenakshi and Jey either!

"When we drive into a city or small town on our Bullet, many heads turn and eyebrows are raised. Sometimes, it is also difficult to have the families agree with our concept and let us into their house in return of making an art work for them," he reveals. Recollecting some of the not so pleasant episodes, they tell us about families who had not been able to adjust to the idea of strangers living in their house, or them calling the media to get local coverage. And yet, the matured learning on their faces is enough revelation to explain how they have grown and each unfavourable situation has been a lesson. Since their modes of transport are their two-wheelers Hari Bhari and Kesariya, the couple also often face the apprehension and fear of friends and well-wishers, along with the mistrust of strangers. Some would believe it to be crazy and unsafe. This couple, however, as firm believers of their gut feelings, have found beautiful journeys unfold with these companions. With determination and organization, the couple has so far managed pretty well between their conventional career and family schedule to make way for their innovative endeavour. Thankfully, there hasn't been interference or discouragement from close friends or family, who have let the duo swim through the tides. However, time and money do pose to be a major challenge; a fact that the couple is aware of and still contemplating a solution.

"We really wish we had the luxury of time. Between Jey's job and my schedules, there are only so many days we can take out for Artologue's actual travel. The money also goes from our own pockets for a lot of logistics and resources," Meenakshi admits.

An idea so creative and a passion so productive is yet to meet its full potential due to the lack of these provisions. Even though this creative couple has not yet become full time travel artists which limits their reach and growth, they compensate by every possible means.

Spending a day with the artsy couple will show you the various textures that help them form Artologue. Breathing, thinking and living art, the couple spends time connecting with people who have been past associates or have future potential. Every minute of the day, when not engaged in the usual routine, is spent building plans or exploring possibilities for the next places to travel and people to meet. One may wonder whether this transcends the line of work and home, art and living.

"Everything we believe in is right here at Artologue. You can say that this is both our personal and professional expression," Meenakshi speaks with contentment.

Which is why, despite differences and diversions, the two always support each other through thick and thin. With out of the box achievements like bringing several aspiring artists together on the platform of Artwalle, being recognized by some very prestigious organizations of the country, and being the epitome of art on-the-go, these founders of Artologue have come a long way only with the support and co-operation of one another.

"That is one of the biggest benefits of marrying your best friend. Not only do you know each other inside out, but you can expect each other to be there unconditionally," Meenakshi expresses gratefully. In the face of adversities, the two have looked out for each other. However, this does not discredit their individuality, in fact, only accentuates the same. This unique coupling of creativity and logic, macro management with attention to details, silent observation and social engagement has helped Artologue accomplish even the most seemingly impossible projects.

"Simply knowing each other's strengths and weaknesses gives us a certain kind of assurance and also a signal of the way forward. We know how to make the best use of this opportunity. I think that is what has brought us so far," she adds.

Looking back fondly at the roller coaster ride that has been their journey with Artologue, the couple recollects their exhibition as Artwalle as one of their biggest recognitions. Not only had they managed to bring about two thousand people together to create art on a pair of 16 x 25 feet canvas, but also marked a big step towards the revolution they have set out to create through art.

"It was an enigmatic experience to see so many people come together and spread love and happiness with their sheer presence. It has been one of the most humbling experiences for us, at the same time elevating to see our mission of democratizing art come to reality," Jey speaks beaming with pride.

Not only did this event held in October 2015 serve as a big boost to their morale, but also proved to give them a bigger platform of recognition. Since being placed on the Indian map with their path-breaking idea, Artologue has had several prestigious offers and requests to pursue. The couple takes their decisions about such pursuits with great deliberation and dedication.

"Thankfully, we haven't had to go in search of projects or sell ourselves to potential opportunities. Our work and experiences so far have been noted and talked about by people who matter, and that itself has been enough for people to reach out to us to work for them," Meenakshi explains. "I guess this also has to do with the spirit and energy that we work with. Jey and I firmly believe that in this quest to spread beauty around, good things are bound to happen around us too!"

Couple, partners, co-travellers – these are but a few words that may describe the equation that this duo shares. However, if one sets to explore the nature of their vision, their accomplishments and the journey so far, one may find it difficult to put it down in words. For some, they have been artwalle, for others they have been an opportunity to experience something different. During this journey, they have made some art and they have made some friends. From learning about art and places, to learning about people and about themselves, Meenakshi and Jey have come a long way in the quest of their passion. With something that may have originated with the selfish motive of doing what they love, they have selflessly achieved something that has benefitted many people from different geographies and backgrounds. In Artologue, the duo finds their vocation and their avocation, their passion and their romance, their individuality and their togetherness. Not only have they managed to bring about a story to leave you starry-eyed, but also turned circumstances into real accomplishments, giving art a new meaning for people who may have been made to believe that it wasn't for them. Artologue is a display of the exemplary spirit of life that fills all our canvases with colours.

To colour yourself in their passion and bring out the arty side in you, visit www.artologue.in or their Facebook page /Artologue: Art for all.

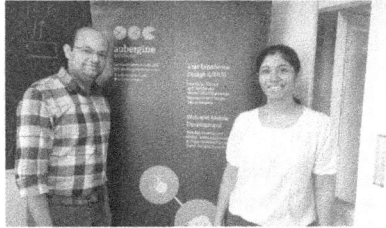

"Love and work can go hand in hand, when your life partner becomes your business partner."

Vishal & Preeti *hold degrees in commerce and design, and management, respectively. But their love for art and will to make it happen led to their founding* **ArtZolo,** *an online portal that helps artists and art lovers buy and sell original art at affordable prices.*

Partners in Art – ARTZOLO

By Preeti & Vishal

Two families moved from their traditional north Indian environment to the southern culture of India. Both for the reason of trade, and moulded themselves into the multicultural set-up of the new ambience. Both crossed paths in a social gatherings and that led to the foundation of a conglomeration of families, with their son and daughter getting married. Thus, a man and a woman, from Haryana and Rajasthan, respectively, came together in nuptial ties, leading to the beginning of not only a relationship based on love, faith and undying commitment, but also to set an example of companionship beyond home.

When such relationships come to life, something extraordinary is produced. And when the equation grows beyond the mere domestic, something far more productive and meaningful is formed. More often than not, such companionship creates ripples that affect more than just the couple. An environment is created that allows for more people to benefit from it. It is love stories like these that become inspiration for others to learn and follow. It wasn't a typical love story though, that sprouted when two people met and decided to get married. Here, in fact, the boy wed the girl and that's how their journey of discovering each other, their love, talents and aspirations began.

After a bachelor's degree in software engineering, Vishal worked for four years before moving to Toronto to for his master's degree in business administration. Having acquired in-depth understanding of strategies, he worked as a business strategist in a reputed firm. On the other hand, Preeti holds degrees in commerce and interior designing. After completing her education, she joined her family business and helped running it. With a detailed understanding of the diverse aspects of enterprise, she gained experiences of operation, finances, consumer behaviour, etc. With such diversity of experiences and interests, the two individuals who had come together through marriage, became partners at work by what we may call a stroke of destiny.

As Vishal decided to continue the legacy of his entrepreneurial gene, he faced a few massive challenges in the first year of his endeavour. It was a time when he was in the process of building his startup and met hiccups that were difficult to resolve. Preeti, besides her experience in the family business, also held affection and sensitivity towards her husband's situation and stood strong as a pillar of support. Eventually, she decided to extend her backing from emotional to professional as well. This is how out of love and mutual understanding, the foundation of the partnership was laid down, that led to the eventuality of a flourishing business. Complementing each other with their respective skills and experience, they finally started their own startup in the year 2014 that came to be known as ArtZolo.

The concept of ArtZolo had germinated in the Innovation and Incubation Center of IIT Kanpur in early 2014. Vishal, who had been smitten with the entrepreneurial bug since his days in the US, had been diligently researching about the market gap and opportunities in the Indian space. His study led him to identify education and art as two major dimensions of opportunities that had not yet been explored to their optimal potential. Up to date with the rising trend of 'dotcoms', Vishal's inference led him to corner an online venture with art. And with this principle concept, ArtZolo continued to materialize with the mutual co-operation of the two.

As an online portal with its reach and scale spread in different cities of the country, ArtZolo works on the concept of providing a platform for artwork of different artists who otherwise may not find visibility and exposure in a large audience. Various artists take membership with the venture and put up high resolution images of their work on the online portal. The collections are then displayed as a virtual exhibition. The exhibition is open for viewers to see and select from, and to place purchase orders. Once a customer has the final artwork delivered to their doorstep and is satisfied with their work, the payment is released to the artist. To ensure no plagiarism, artist watermarks are placed on each piece put up on display. Thus, in an effective, efficient and transparent manner, the entire transaction is carried out, with benefit for all the parties involved.

"Apart from buying the artwork, customers can also bid on high demand products which are put up for auction, thus giving a real life auction house feel. Most of our revenue comes from the commission from art sales, ranging between 15% and 30% of the value. An artist can sell either open or limited edition prints on the site," explains Vishal about the functionality of the enterprise.

Within a year of functionality, ArtZolo found itself gaining recognition amidst its clientele. However, this successful struggle comes from a beginning that has seen its share of struggles and difficulties.

"The beginning was a struggle in itself. Having had experiences that had been bitter, we were both very apprehensive about taking each step."

During testing times, both the entrepreneurial as well as familial ties were put to test for the couple. Narrowing down the categories of art that were to be included in business, keeping in mind how practical in terms of procurement and transaction they would be, were tough decisions to make. Post this, connecting with various artists and bringing them onboard with the idea was a challenge in itself.

"The concept of online exhibitions and sending their paintings first and receiving money later was something that was unheard of for the artists. It took a lot of faith-building to make them understand the benefit of this model," explains Preeti in retrospection. Moreover, building an online portal that would be both user-friendly as well as attractive in appearance had to be looked into with great detail. Connecting this with a safe payment portal was also to be done cautiously. Since these were elements that were being done for the first time by both Vishal and Preeti, it kept them on their toes in the initial phase. Having financial liberty to explore was not a luxury with ArtZolo, because they were both managing with their cash reserves. Without this cushion, money spent in important areas like technology or marketing were cut short at many instances.

"We could have found a bigger and better boost had money matters been more favourable. Hence, to take each step with most cost effective angle was a big challenge for us," she goes on to explain. However, with a positive spirit and persistent attitude, the duo went on to make the most of each challenge and emerge with significant achievements and learnings to their credit. As a result, ArtZolo grew on to flourish and find stability and success, month after month. Expressing their journey so far as a terrific experience, the two talk about the ups and downs they have faced in business together. Not only does this give them an opportunity to deal with artists, but also a chance to connect with personalities they love. It is this affection and passion integrated with their skills that have helped the dynamic duo scale up and reach a stage where they are connected with artisans from across the country.

Giving credit where it's due is in the humble nature of both Vishal and Preeti.

"We found immense support from friends and family. There were times when we were stuck taking a decision or were in a financial crisis. But they stood by us and helped us out as best as they could," Vishal accepts with affection.

Equally significant in this journey has been the mutual trust and cooperation between the husband and wife that has helped them evolve as partners as well as individuals through the course of this entrepreneurial journey. After the initial collaboration of handling everything together, where roles and responsibilities were often overlapping, the couple bifurcated into their respective verticals of strengths and expertise. This not only helps them make independent decisions, but also catalyses the process of efficient execution. With a candid expression, Preeti goes on to explain the nuances of this equation, "Of course this comes with its own baggage. Having spent so much time with each other, not only do we understand each other's strengths, but also the differences we have with each other."

Keeping the delicate balance between partnership and individuality, they realize the probabilities of how easy it is for things to go wrong and affect both the personal and professional front. Identifying both the opportunity and risk that stands in their way, the two offer each other their undying commitment and yet maintain the space of their individuality that helps them to learn and evolve with each challenge and accomplishment.

Speaking of accomplishments so far, Vishal proudly talks about the short and significant progress they have made within a year of being operational. At the time when the business was finding its first toddling steps, there were uncertainties whether the idea that was brilliant in concept would also ace on practical grounds.

"We did not have credibility back then and were almost desperate to prove ourselves. Our first international client came by around that time. Not only did this bring in great business, but was also symbolic both for our potential as well as future prospects. I felt very proud at that moment," he reflects with excitement. Counting every achievement with due respect and utilizing it as a method to boost themselves and the team, ArtZolo nourishes a culture of gratitude and celebration.

"I remember the day we were featured on the front page of *The Times of India,* Chennai edition. It was a mark of recognition and also did wonders for our business," she adds with a sense of satisfaction. What started with an idea in the incubation centre, has today found a physical shape and form of success. Having expanded in scale and reach, with time, ArtZolo has also extended its strength to a seven-member team.

"We are a family of like-minded individuals who believe in a common cause. I think that, and our passion, keeps us going strong together," adds Preeti. With categorical focus on areas of strength, ArtZolo is looking forward to future expansions with plans that are under construction at the moment. As people with an evolutionary bent of mind, the duo concentrates on making the best use of their strengths in business and do not believe in competitive comparisons. "There may be indirect competition around us, but our attention is solely on our own success at the moment," Vishal talks with insight.

As a couple that spends most of their time involved with work, Vishal and Preeti have flexible boundaries between work and home.

"Sometimes holidays are dedicated to business, but often, time spent at work is also contributing to us coming close as a married couple," Preeti speaks with a smile.

With advice for many aspiring entrepreneurs, both as individuals as well as a couple, they talk about having their priorities clear and holding the maturity to handle the space that people share as professional partners. With honesty and transparency, support and strong commitment is also a mantra to succeeding in business, according to the enterprising pair. Not only have Vishal and Preeti set an example of what commitment and mutual trust can lead to, but have also managed to break the myth that personal relations cannot mature into a professional partnership. Having identified the opportunity among Indian artists, ArtZolo today stands as exemplary for taking the leap of faith and finding success in what life offers to you instead of simply holding on to the challenges and complaining about the failures.

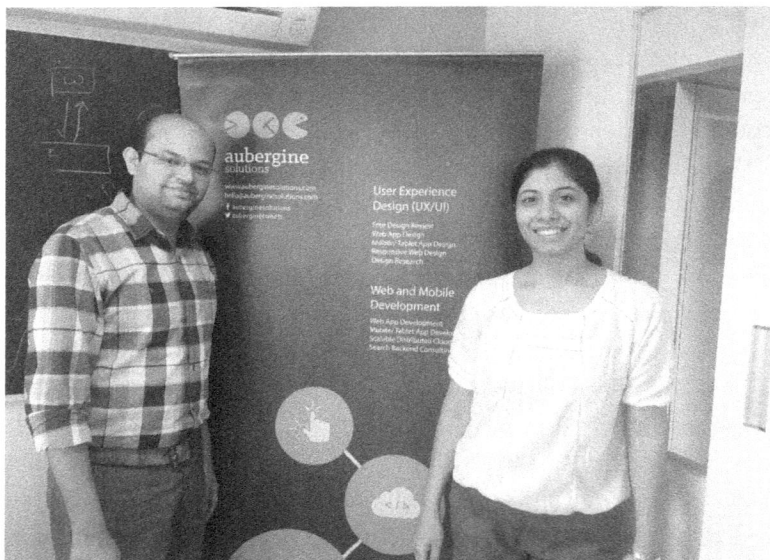

Smartly amalgamating information technology, computer science and design, **Sarthak & Bhakti** *gave wings to* **Aubergine Solutions** *to provide services in publishing, consultancy and supply of various kinds of software to enable ease of use and experience across all strata of life.*

The Specifics of a Partnership – AUBERGINE SOLUTIONS

By Sarthak & Bhakti

Both enormously qualified in the fields of information-technology and computer science, as well as design, Sarthak and Bhakti had been studying together for four years, and had been extremely good friends. They decided to take their friendship a step further, because their connection went beyond the classroom. Sharing a deep passion for information technology and a common streak for innovation, the duo clicked on multiple levels – both on the professional as well as personal front. After completing their graduation, they started dating each other, while pursuing their own individual career paths. While Bhakti moved to Gujrat to attain her master's degree in design, Sarthak transported to the US to pursue his master's degree in computer science. Through testing times, that came with its own share of ups and downs, the duo continued a long distance relationship, got engaged and after a prolonged courtship of two years, got married in 2008.

The couple continued to pursue their passion of information technology, gaining a myriad experiences in corporates, startups and firms in the Silicon Valley. While a fresh perspective in the US market allowed them a privilege of experiencing some of the most innovative software services and user interfaces, they also continuously realized the gap between the opportunity and quality of services of such domains being offered in the Indian market.

"It was partly due to our passion for continuously evolving in this sector, and partly the visibility of a huge enterprising gap, just waiting to be explored in the Indian market, that caught our immediate attention," Sarthak speaks about the sparking idea.

That the couple would engineer this idea into a ventured opportunity does not come as a big surprise. It was the most obvious course of direction for the duo passionate about engineering and innovation, and bitten by the entrepreneurial bug. Sarthak had already got his share of experience and knowledge about the nitty-gritty of a startup's functionality. And consequently, it didn't take a lot of convincing when Bhakti pitched the idea for them to consider starting something on their own, catering to the Indian market.

"There were certainly some moments of self-doubt – it was a big decision, after all, and there were too many things at stake. But it was Bhakti's conviction that had me completely bowled over in agreement," he reveals candidly.

Although the larger aim was to address the situation in their homeland, Bhakti had already begun working for Indian clients while still stationed in the US. While the couple admits that the decision of moving back home had surfaced in their discussions before, it was just a matter of 'when' that big decision had to be taken. However, the experience during the initiation cleared all doubts in their heads about this critical choice.

"Our very first client came in for a user experience design project, which we delivered while based out of the US. Thankfully, it was a huge success. And that's what got us tempted to calculate, that if we could achieve something like this from so far away, the consequence of hands on involvement while at the location in India would be incredible!" Bhakti reminisces.

Thus, a fate-changing decision was made by the couple and they moved back to India to start actualizing their dream. Even after making the decision, it is appreciable that their journey began with maturity and categorical planning. While Bhakti moved back to India immediately to set up base in Vadodara, Sarthak stayed back for a period of three months, all this while working aggressively towards spreading the word about the new business. The strategy helped them considerably in bringing new leads with business opportunities. Thus, hardwork channeled back and forth in their venture, and soon Sarthak and Bhakti formulated their enterprise in February 2013, giving it the swanky name of Aubergine Solutions.

"If you have to appeal to people, you have to be attractive, in a way that catches their attention. Aubergine is a very specific colour – it's different from the genre. Extremely detailed and specific answers to the problems is what we provide," Bhakti explains.

Offering a unique selling point of product innovation with experience, the couple defines their service as committed and creative. Dedicated to designing software products for web and mobile applications, Aubergine Solutions amalgamates the product and service quality of Silicon Valley, along with the customization according to Indian needs. This coupled with a detailed understanding of the gaps in other services not only gave them a head start, but an obvious upper edge over any other companies offering user experience solutions.

Having been functional for the almost three years, Aubergine Solutions has seen significant development in its growth, client acquisition, diversity in portfolio and all the experience that the venture has picked up in all this while. However, it would be unfair to say that the journey has been hunky dory for the two. In fact, the sheer magnitude of challenges they have faced in this short span has brought them to a remarkable level.

"The very idea of moving back to India was the most difficult decision we have had to make," Sarthak comments. "Although the excitement of starting something on our own was a motivation, to know that this could backfire massively is something we couldn't have ruled out."

Not only was relocating a high risk decision, but putting everything they had saved into this enterprise also raised the stakes significantly. However, the more trying times came in only after this phase of initiation had passed. Aubergine Solutions had initially been stationed at Vadodara in Gujrat. With the passage of time, the co-founders realized that this decision, which had been taken with the the luxury of network and family support in mind, led to the problem of the lack of human resources, because not many suitable persons for the kind of profiles they were seeking could come to work in the city. Thus, for the second time, and timely so, they shifted base to Ahmedabad, where they were sure to find bigger exposure, better people, and more effective visibility. While challenges on the professional front were helping them gain experience, developments on the personal front also kept the couple on their toes! Bhakti's pregnancy and eventual motherhood in the very early phase of the business development put the duo in a fix between excitement and stress. In a very short span, they would need to find someone who could help them in Bhakti's absence. After diligent searching and experienced insight, they managed to bring somebody on board who went on to become a strong pillar of support in the enterprise. The struggles that the couple has seen only symbolize their victory in the face of challenges each time, encouraging them to take further risks in the path of growth. With mettle to beat the odds without the slightest loss in conviction, this couple has not only carved a niche in the vast enterprising sea of the country, but also managed to show tremendous promise for evolution with changing times. With passing years, more and more individuals seem to be breaking away from their jobs to set up something of their own – big or small. In an already fierce race of competitors, this phenomenon seems to be creating a lot of strain. However, the brilliant and ambitious co-founders of Aubergine Solutions show little fear regarding the issue.

"Understandably, there is a lot of competition. But why should that stop you from excelling at everything that you are good at? In fact, it is a brilliant idea to get out of your comfort zone and survive amidst excellence. That's what keeps you on the edge, hungry for getting better each time," Sarthak's conviction radiates blindingly.

The most influential source of encouragement in the face of the struggles has been an unconditional support that the two have offered each other. In times where competitive ambitions spoil even the best of friendships, having each other to fall back on has been a strong source of strength. Not only does sharing a partnership with each other give them a sense of relief and understanding, but this unique equation has also empowered Sarthak and Bhakti in a complementing manner.

"Between the two of us, there are not defined set of roles. It's a pure continuum of dedication and contribution of everything we have known or learned," Bhakti speaks with maturity. Bringing forth a diverse plate of expertise between the two of them, both the co-founders cover different verticals of the business. While aiming for the best achievement of their independent domains, it is impossible to separate one's contribution from the other.

"We have our independence and yet there's this incredible sense of partnering up with each other. Our perspectives, our decisions and even our challenges are entwined with one another," Sarthak speaks fondly. But if that puts you under the illusion that the two walk the same track every single moment, he is also quick to correct you right there. "It's not like there are no differences. Of course there are times when our opinions or decisions clash. But that's where the true colours of a relationship show, right?"

Speaking of differences and boundaries, looking at the two through their day at work, it is hard to say where the personal ends and the professional begins for them. The same charisma and dedication floats in their very essence, whether they're syncing up with team members at the beginning of the day, connecting with clients, or completing tasks with the minutest details. And if you thought that was all, you haven't seen them with their son! A powerhouse of energy, this family bustles with excitement and participation in all tasks, big or small, together. Despite being a couple that broke away from conventions and gave up on stable, lucrative jobs to start something so unpredictable, their own families have been extremely supportive and encouraging. Striking a remarkable balance between home and work, the duo revels in the moments they spend either discussing the latest developments in their lives, or cherishing the fun their child shares with them.

Looking back, Sarthak reflects on all things that have happened. Ask him if there were mistakes and he proudly says none. Before you mistake his forthrightness as arrogance, he wins you over with optimism. "Opportunities come as both success and failure. While success brings you encouragement and increases your bandwidth to reach for more, failures help you work harder on the foundation – the details," he speaks insightfully. Having come this far from a mere idea, today Aubergine Solution stands with an effective and dedicated team of twenty members, a plethora of projects to their credit and a hat full of accomplished feathers.

"Working with the Aubergine team made us realize the value and benefit of effective user interface and experience. Their approach is thorough, research oriented and focused on goals and deliverables, making them an integral part of any team they work with," speaks Hardik Parikh, co-founder of a reputed firm that is a loyal client of the enterprise.

Quoted by many as a highly recommended place for excellent service, Aubergine Solutions is also known for being a benign platform to learn and grow. While at one level, this strongly resonates the commitment of the founders, it is also an important commentary on the work culture that the organization creates.

"I think it is about what you love. When work no longer remains an obligation but becomes something you like dedicating your time to, something that feels worth all the effort, you know you are doing it right!" exclaims Bhakti with a generous smile.

Celebrating everything as a team and as a couple keep these shining entrepreneurs motivated. For individuals who have accomplished so much in a considerably short span of time, the duo is extremely grounded and humble. Looking out for each other, both Sarthak and Bhakti speak of having become better persons in this journey. An example of a healthy, cooperative and respectful relationship, they have evolved both professionally and personally in the process. Acclaiming each other's support and faith for the success they have achieved, the couple envisages becoming the de-facto name on everyone's lips when they think of user interface and experience solutions. With such a symbiotic support system, impeccable partnership and a quality that surpasses expectation, there is no doubt that this enterprising couple has a long way to go. Along the way, of course, they have become an ideal example to follow.

---

aubergine
solutions

For customised software solutions that work like wonders, you can reach them at www.auberginesolutions.com or on Facebook at /auberginesolutions.

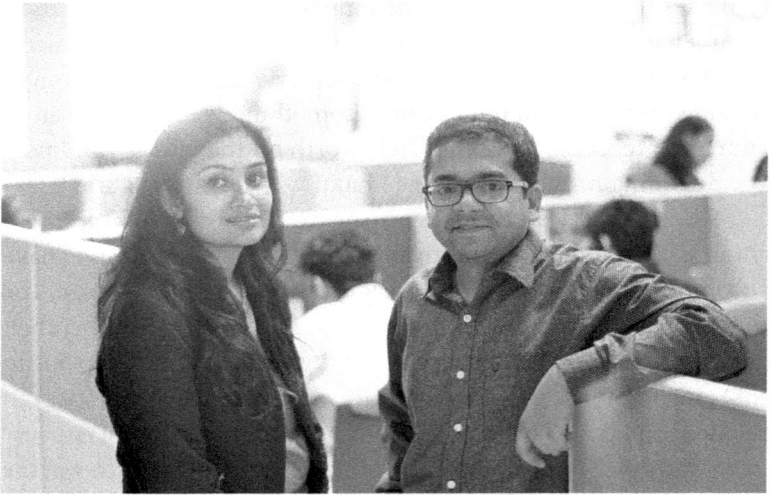

In a bid to do something revolutionary in the realm of communication, with a planned approach to help startups grow and make a place for themselves in the mainstream, **Aakriti & Anshul** *came up with the idea of* **Boring Brands** *- a communication and marketing consultancy.*

Partnering through Life –
BORING BRANDS

By Aakriti & Anshul

Many long-lasting love stories begin as college romances and theirs was no exception. Attraction evolved into affection and that led to a simple forever. However, their partnership was more than just love and their relationship was more than just about each other. She was a master of expression; he was the king of technology. And together they built a story worth telling.

Drawing inspiration from their story, one of the most reputed companies of communications in India was set up. Anshul, having graduated from one of the best engineering colleges of the country, had already gained respect and fame with his live projects he had made as a student for some of the top brands of the country. A go-getter from the start, Anshul was someone who had both the respect and confidence of his batch-mates. A romantic at heart, he was an ambitious guy who always aspired to do something that could impact lives around. Aakriti, on the other hand, was a fresher from a premier college of Delhi University. Their paths crossed at a ragging session where Aakriti was being introduced to the seniors and Anshul watched on, struck by her spirited air. Leaving no stone unturned to win her love, the lover boy tried everything from mid-night deliveries to hacking her emails. As destiny would have it, Aakriti finally fell in love with him, and they came to be known as one of the most memorable couples of their times. After four years of being together, Anshul and Aakriti tied the knot in December 2008.

But this is not a love story about the dynamic duo. It is in fact a story about everything after that, that this enterprising couple built with their own hands. Having worked on projects through their post-graduation, the couple was well aware of each other's skills and strengths. It was indeed their dream to take this relationship a step further and start something together, in a way that they both found gratification. Having worked their ways up the professional ladder, working for the most reputed brands in the country, the two found themselves yearning for something exciting and productive.

"Aakriti wanted to do something revolutionary in the realm of communication; it was something floating in her head all the time," recollects Anshul.

As someone who has shown unquestioned support to his wife, he went on to encourage her through the risk-laden steps she was taking.

"He was a little apprehensive initially, but he never tried to hold me back," recalls Aakriti fondly. "All he asked me was if I'd be able to make about five thousand a month!"

It was perhaps this unconditional support that encouraged Aakriti to quit her job and start an enterprise dedicated to her ambition of changing the way communication works in the country. This led to the foundation of what would later become one of the most unique and efficient organizations dedicated specifically to the needs of new age startup organizations in the country. The couple built together BoringBrands – an agency that has today become a one stop solution for all advertising and marketing needs of the fast-catching startup trend in India. Since its inception, BoringBrands has worked with more than a hundred and seventy-five startups across a realm of verticals who raised over $900 million in funding (and counting).

Back in 2009, small organizations were only beginning to set base across verticals. To the two dedicated professionals, it was more than evident that there was neither an efficient system to cater to the needs of such startups, nor accessible guidance for them. In most cases, unprofessional help was being hired for low cost and this led to disastrous results. Gauging the potential growth of this sector and the significant gap that needed to be addressed, Aakriti and Anshul built BoringBrands with the mission of acting as the perfect platform to help such newbies stabilize in the fierce and competitive industry. Inspired by the words of Gandhi – be the change you want to see in the world – Aakriti talks about the embodiment and the spirit in their organization. Summing up the aim and objective of the enterprise, Anshul explains,

"It's all about leveraging the power of marketing as a growth engine for a brand."

Pitching their unique selling point categorically, the couple explains that in BoringBrands, every act, decision and strategy is connected with the vision of their client's business growth; even weekly Facebook posts are all about that. In a crowd of agencies that focus on merely making poster impressions of the brand amidst the mob of advertisements, BoringBrands is dedicated to a harmonious projection of translating every action into progressive results.

"We encourage an integrated work strategy, where everyone knows what everyone else is doing. This helps to build a holistic and complimentary machinery, instead of mere fragmented assignments," explains Aakriti insightfully. Today the company works with startups not just in India, but across the world, including United States, Canada, Australia and Singapore and this is just the beginning!

One might wonder though, why such an unconventional name for such an insightful enterprise!

"When we formulated this company, we didn't want to be like any other usual PR or digital marketing company. We wanted to create brands in ways nobody had tried before. Our approach and strategy would always be experimental, cool and out-of-the-box. We didn't want to restrict ourselves to doing just one thing. Our essence was quirk and we wanted to have a name that had an underlying spirit of global rebellion attached to it; hence BoringBrands," smiles Anshul.

❖

With a name so whacky, catchy and yet deeply appropriate with reference to the solutions they offer, BoringBrands stands as a consistent favourite for many organizations that are starting up their business from across verticals. Explaining the intention behind dedicating themselves to the needs of newbies, Aakriti puts the motivation into words,

"Startups are, by nature, fast-growing and solving the pain in the society which is not solved by the conventional and traditional companies, and hence they are the ones spawning new industries."

Furthering their in-depth understanding of how this sprouting industry works, she lays down that the dynamics of a startup are different and hence the marketing of such a company cannot be a copy-paste job from the marketing plan of a big company. It has to cater to their specific outcome. Unlike the popular belief about startups having less money, BoringBrands fundamentally believes that the newly set-up organizations, in fact, have the right money to do exactly what is needed, and with the strategy hitting home, they have what it takes to raise money for the next level.

"Startups come with a pro-risk approach and things are a lot more transparent and crisp. This is a challenging and yet extremely exciting way of working that we at BoringBrands not only understand but also cater to."

With an aim to create big brands, not merely manage them, the couple stood out with determination during a time when startups were looked down upon. In a space where the giants dominate and run business on the sole credential of years of holding up, it was a challenge for the new startups to even find recognition. In such difficult times, Boring Brands stood out as the perfect solution with an organized and experienced solution system, with due respect and sensitivity to the needs and limitations of the organizations that were just starting out.

However, unlike what looks like the successful establishment of BoringBrands today, the initial struggles of the enterprise were significant milestones in bringing them this far.

"Many people had said it was an awful idea to work with your spouse, that married life would also be affected," reveals Aakriti. However, with mutual respect and understanding of each other's style of working, the couple was more than ready to break the traditional warning and take their leap of faith with each other.

"The biggest challenge came for us when we became parents and had to juggle between taking care of our child and the business – both in their nascent stages of life," Aakriti reflects thinking about the most testing time of her life.

"It was a litmus test for both the business and the family. We went through crunched timelines, and speedy hiring processes. I think it was a lesson in management."

It was also an uncertain move for them to quit their stable jobs despite financial obligation that launching into a new venture would involve. Since working with startups had its own share of uncertainties in terms of their sustainability, scale of investment and client retention, etc., to find reliable and motivated team members and to have them commit to dealing with the dynamics of starting up organizations was paramount. The duo had to learn the hard way about the importance of curating and sustaining the right talent for the right business growth.

However, the qualities of perseverance and the humility to accept mistakes wherever necessary have brought the co-founders of BoringBrands a long way. The enterprise has overcome its biggest challenges and made its talent its core competency. Striking the best chords with their clients, this creative enterprise has reached an exemplary zenith of success with seven years of experience and over a hundred and seventy-five loyal clients. Identifying the journey so far as something of an inspiring stimulation, Anshul talks about each day at work as being a new experience,

"Every new client, every new assignment is an experience full of learning. Through this journey, we have met some of the most awe-inspiring and creative people from diverse walks of life. This is one of the biggest incentives of working with many creative and dynamic startups." One of the most influential turning points for the venture came when a reputed international brand approached the duo to help building their marketing strategy. Although BoringBrands had been stabilizing slowly and steadily with consistent work, having a global brand decorating their portfolio came with a gush of multiple organizations approaching them with work. Amidst the clustered space of agencies, word of mouth for the uprising enterprise spread with goodwill, and ever since, there has been no looking back! Having a deep rooted connect with the Indian startup ecosystem, BoringBrands has worked closely with investors such as IDG Ventures and startups backed by the likes of Tiger Global, Sequoia Capital, Accel Partners and Nirvana ventures, amongst others. Some of the clients they have worked with include OYO Rooms, CashKaro, Aspiring Minds, Mavin, Uniphore, Udacity, LinkedIn and many more."

❖

Speaking categorically of their business model, the entrepreneurial couple explains how they extend marketing expertise for business growth of the newbies. Services ranging from strategy designing to advertisement production are all offered for the entrepreneurs kick-starting their business. As a brand dedicated to startups, they believe in planning at least six months ahead of their tasks in sync with the dynamism of the client's need. This is why BoringBrands is doing well in technology, catering to the most effective and efficient technological advantages that today's marketing platforms offer. They believe in evolving their mechanism every now and then. In this uniqueness, Anshul explains, they have their in-house product where clients can log in to see the work in progress, rather than waiting for an Excel sheet in their mailbox.

Customizing to the most detailed needs of the clientele, BoringBrand offers marketing solutions that are tailor-made and boasts this as not only a model of their expertise, but also exclusivity. Speaking of a work culture that specializes to this advanced need of new age business, Aakriti explains the categorical yet holistically inclined work roles of each team member. A team of sixty, that is fast expanding its skills and number, is deeply motivated with a value system and mutual respect.

"The mantra of work here is empowerment. Smartness and sharpness is respected and encouraged, while independent creativity and decision-making is rooted in work. This is what keeps us motivated to push ourselves and do better each time," she exclaims proudly.

Even as partners at work, the couple marks their roles according to their strengths and interests. While Aakriti takes care of communication, and supports in the commerce aspects of the enterprise, Anshul dedicates his skills for marketing strategies and process management of the organization. This equilibrium functions on the grounds of deep understanding and respect for each other's decisions and space – qualities hard to find even in the most professional partnerships.

Just like their synergy at work, Aakriti and Anshul share a symbiotic bond in their personal life as well. Whether it is about raising their three-year-old son, taking care of domestic and familial needs of one another, or simply spending time to unwind and evolve, the couple strives to find the perfect balance. With each day full of targets, goals and deadlines, they still make it a point to relax and rejuvenate, spending time as a family, where their son becomes the center of their attention and affection. So much so, that the young one in the family has already become a familiar member of the team, as he is often found spending time at BoringBrands, bringing a breath of fresh air or ideating inspiration for the think tanks at work!

"Our key to success, both as a couple as well as partners in business, is that we have stuck to being partners in everything we do. Whether it is facing challenges, making decisions or celebrating success, we have complemented each other through every spec and spectrum. I guess that's why we have made it so far!" Aakriti reveals with a candid smile.

As a couple, they have achieved many milestones of success that have made them proud of their initial decision. From acquiring their first client, to setting up their first office and giving a physical form to their passion, each moment has been cherished. Although comfortable and secured with their accomplishments, plans of expansion include not only bringing in some of the most promising startups to the Indian market, but also diversifying in their product portfolio with technological advancements. BoringBrands simply does not recognize competition, for the sheer reason that there is none! While many agencies have started catering to startups as an add-on today, there is none like the expertise of BoringBrands that is acting as a platform for business growth.

Aakriti and Anshul make a story that is told to many...but not simply as a romance that blossomed in the corridors of college, but as an evolution they marked together with the brilliance of their partnership. Defying myths, and breaking conventions, the duo go on to dismiss the myth that couples can't be partners outside of home, and acclaim that with perfect understanding and respect, they make the best examples to follow, both in their personal life, as well as their professional endeavours.

If you have a product or organisation that needs to be seen and talked about, Boring Brands is the place to be. Visit www.boringbrands.com, or catch them on Facebook at /boringbrands.

Swati & Rohan *love to shop and they have made shopping experience for people across India an even better experience with attractive cashback deals.* **CashKaro.com** *is a one stop shop for attractive deals on leading brands and e-commerce websites.*

The Best Deal from the Best Partners – CASHKARO.COM

By Swati & Rohan

When the best scholars of one the best institutes in the world meet, something extraordinary is bound to happen. Whether this makes for a story that changes economics or dynamics, it is sure to affect hundreds of people. Such is the journey of Swati and Rohan. As fellow mates in the London School of Economics, dating partners, husband and wife or business partners, the duo has carved a niche for themselves. In fact, not just for themselves but also for the people in the country.

After being awarded a scholarship to undertake an Honor's degree in Mathematics and Economics, Swati moved to London to complete her graduation. From college, she moved to one of the most reputed organizations in investment banking, working closely with the CO-CEOs of the brand. She absorbed the best for the next five years of her career. Rohan had moved to England from the US, also to study at the London School of Economics. Like Swati, he too started his career right after college and went on to work with an asset management fund. With his skills and tact, he grew the asset base from $50 million to $750 million in just over five years! Moving on, he joined a large US-based hedge fund and led a billion dollar acquisition and worked there for two years. This exponential growth was a reflection of nothing less than exemplary hard work and skills on Rohan's part.

The two had met in college and were friends. With similar interests and ideas, the two started dating each other while still in college. After dating for an year, Swati and Rohan decided to get married, and tied the knot in 2009.

The couple had already accomplished a lot in terms of experience and credibility, apart from gathering a network of some of the best entrepreneurs in the sector. And thus, with such accomplishments to their credit, they decided to divert their energy and skills from working for other firms to building something substantial for themselves. Venturing into the world of entrepreneurship, they built a B2B Cashback Loyalty solutions model called Pouring Pounds in UK. With adequate experience and understanding of the area, they soon minted the success of their model in the country, only to realize that opportunities back home were aplenty. With the rising e-commerce trend and market in India, they gauged the potential of the upsurge which is claimed to reach a scale of becoming a $100 billion industry by the year 2020.

"We understand the innate Indian love for saving and making the best deal, and we realized that no one has ever made the best use of this opportunity. This brought us back to India in 2011," recollects Rohan about the turning point in their lives.

In April 2013, with principally the same model that had been tried and tested in Pouring Pounds, the couple launched their brain child in India as an exclusive cashback service in B2B. Thus, the entrepreneurial journey for Swati and Rohan began in India.

"Both Rohan and I have been consistent users of cashback sites ourselves and understand the nuances and nerves that such portals work on. But starting something like this in India was an entirely different ballgame," explains Swati.

With Rohan initiating the idea, the duo worked on the concept of creating and building on the concept with its several affiliates. Thus, with deep understanding, sincere hard work, and smart collaborations, Swati and Rohan brought to life what we now have come to know and love as CashKaro. As India's largest cashback and coupons site, CashKaro functions on the affiliate model and allows its members to get up to thirty percent extra cashback from collaborated brands such as Amazon, Paytm, Snapdeal, Jabong and so on. Dedicated to online transactions, CashKaro is available for anyone who visits the website and then shops through this portal. Consequently, the site receives commission from the respective brands, which is then translated into cashback for its users in the form of real cash! This is the most simple and effective interface for buyers from across the country. What makes it unique and most appreciable is that this extra cashback provided by CashKaro is over and above all coupons, discounts, sales or schemes that the respective brands may be offering to the buyers at any point of time. Unlike most schemes that cancel out on any or all of these privileges, CashKaro caters to the expectations of its users and offers more than the most. With an out of the box model for business, the name in itself is reflective of both the funkiness as well as the simplicity of the service.

"It's simply what we offer – cash is all about real money and *'karo'* in Hindi means action, referring to the actioned opportunities that lie before us. Hence the amalgamation is all about making more cash with just the right action," Swati breaks down the brand to its fundamentals. With its effective direction and transparent simplicity, the brand attracts first time users and succeeds in converting them into loyal customers – an asset which is otherwise hard to keep in today's world of fierce e-commerce opportunities.

Speaking about where all this comes from, Rohan explains his experience with cashback portals in the west with which he has been avidly associated in the past. From first-hand experience, he safely claims that it is possible to help shoppers save worth billions of dollars. However, the concept of cashback was still relatively new back in 2013 when the duo was stepping into the market. As dynamic buyers, the comfort of the known is what makes or breaks a deal for online transactions; this fact was well understood by the masterminds of CashKaro.

"That was one of our biggest challenges: to bring users into a zone of comfort and trust. To convince them that we were reliable and that we were here to bring them profit", Swati recollects. The solution was an aggressive PR and feeding market leaders with the benefits and profits of the model that has already swarmed the west. Unlike conventional opportunities that can be demonstrated with tried and tested examples, this performance-driven model could only be explained in principle in the Indian context, and this is what tested the real mettle of the couple in their will and intelligence to bring together the buy-in of the stalwarts of e-marketing of the country.

While their fears were being addressed on the work front, Swati and Rohan also had several challenges to face in their personal lives. Having their families to understand what they were diving into and how they were absolutely certain and confident about their brain child was a herculean task for the duo.

"To leave stable and lucrative jobs and move to something unpredictable, especially when you are married, is not a very common practice in India, so we could understand the fear of our parents. But it is noteworthy that once they fully understood our concept and witnessed our passion for the work, they went out of their way to shower their blessings and support," Rohan speaks with gratitude.

Then there was the myth that partnering up with your spouse was doomed to end in failure. "There is so much apprehension in people about working with your life partner. If we were not so strong and sure of each other, I am sure, we would have been carried away by this fear ourselves," he confesses honestly. However, having watched each other learn and grow as professionals as well as persons, the dynamic entrepreneurs have placed their unconditional trust in each other. This is what helps them to identify and face challenges together, whether it is at the frontline of work or home.

Having overcome the initial challenges and difficulties of a startup, the couple find contentment and pride in watching their enterprise expand and evolve with every passing stage in the last three years. Being recognized as India's largest cashback site, CashKaro today witnesses an exponential success rate with a safe thirty – forty percent growth rate per month. CashKaro has credited over thirty-five crores as cashback to its members and successfully mobilized over a thousand crores of sales to its affiliated partners. If analytics are to be believed, the site brings together over a million and a half shoppers and the traffic is humongous with CashKaro enabling a cashback to be earned every fifteen seconds! With such a significant achievement by the couple who moved to the country not five years ago, one can only begin to fathom the potential they hold to build and offer to the e-commerce segment of the country.

With a relatively simple and easy business model to speak for this ginormous growth, Rohan speaks about the initiation process of raising the seed funding of USD 750,000 from angel investors.

After seed funding, CashKaro raised twenty-five crores from Kalaari Capital, one of India's leading venture capitalist firms in November 2015. Soon after, in January 2016, Mr. Ratan Tata invested in the company in his personal capacity. With remarkable credentials and a reputation to speak for itself, Swati and Rohan have watched the brand grow from a concept into a full-fledged business that influences the e-commerce traffic in India. Having functioned with a selected and dedicated team of fifteen members only till last year, the organization has grown to seventy-plus members already and is on a constant lookout for dedicated and passionate people to associate with the brand.

"Both Rohan and I are very particular about the kind of people we bring on board and make sure to personally select them on the basis of their skill set, talent and passion," adds Swati with a sense of responsible ownership.

However, more than the dynamism that the comrades in arms share at work, what makes this partnership noteworthy is the unique relationship that Swati and Rohan share and radiate. Despite making the most of their individual strengths and skills, the two do not exhibit any ego or difference in interests, whether it is at the work front or in their personal equation. With utmost respect for each other's independence and intelligence, they have their zones of expertise demarcated.

"Rohan has a technical bent and takes keen interest in product development and innovation. On the other hand, I look after the marketing, communication and investor relations. I love social media, so some of this engagement piece came quite naturally to me. We both took roles that we gravitated to base on our strengths and skills," explains Swati.

With categorical profiles of communications, marketing, PR and finance being tackled at the work front, they do however, support each other in the face of challenges and make sure that neither is ever either overstepping or abandoning the other in their testing times. That, as Swati goes on to explain, has been the key mantra for their success. While the boundary between work and home is more sublime in the case of this enterprising couple, it never comes to affect their equation, as they believe in talking about challenges and differences of opinion rather than keeping it mounted inside their heads and hearts.

"Our time together is focused on making ourselves as individuals and as life partners above and beyond anything else. We are lucky to have each other and to share such a healthy equation, so we never take that for granted," Rohan adds, both with a reflective insight as well as fond affection for Swati.

It is comforting to see that breaking conventions of both professional as well as social boundaries, Swati and Rohan have moved on, not only to establish a business in their country, but also achieved great marks of excellence within a short span of time that they have spent in the Indian market. Defining trust, transparency and truthful communication as the key ingredients in the making of a successful partnership, it is evident that there is more than just being able to work together. As two very accomplished individuals, the couple reflects no signs of ego or arrogance that generally brings down the foundations of most relationships when put to test. With CashKaro as a mere symbol of the strength and success of the real power of such a relationship, Swati and Rohan inspire many rising entrepreneurs to not be afraid of stepping up their relationships and feeling free to explore and appreciate all the strengths of their partners. It is only such holistic bonds that sprout into success, irrespective of whatever segment they delve into!

Flowers and gifts have always been a special way to say you care, and **Sameer & Smriti** *have come together to start up* **Florista** *to make your cherished moments and people feel even more special.*

A Blooming Journey – FLORISTA

By Smriti & Sameer

This might seem like a perfect story for big screen cinema. There's love, there's adventure and a lot of drama too! We have an extrovert and social butterfly who enjoys travelling, pursuing her dreams of a professional career. A smart yet quiet perfectionist who has a creative approach to life and holds a sharp wit with an efficient eye for details continues inconspicuously as a tech guy. But when the two meet, a new story begins, that reaches far beyond the regular boy meets girl one. Smriti and Sameer were batch-mates in their engineering course of graduation and despite their visibly different personalities, became friends on the first day. They were best friends by the final year and eventually started dating after graduating. 'Buddy' is what they call each other even today, when they are married with a happy family. But their relationship stretches beyond the nuptial bond.

With a different set of interests and skills, the couple entered their respective professional careers and continued to gather rich experience in the field – Sameer in creatives and advertising and Smriti in software engineering. However, beneath this layer of seemingly stable professional lives, they knew they had to do something different for themselves; something that would challenge them intellectually and help them evolve an enterprise of their own. Having each other only escalated the process and learning, as they had each other for support and to fall back on and share ideas without inhibitions.

"It was the most natural course of action for us. We didn't have to try to be doing something together. I guess we were just meant to be partners of something bigger than only our marriage," Smriti expresses candidly.

It all began when the entrepreneurial bug hit Sameer, and he quit his job to start Bridge 360 – a full- fledged advertising agency. By 2004, Sameer had already decided that he wanted to start something parallel to his advertising business. And when Smriti heard the idea, she was totally in for it. Gauging the market, they figured a challenging and untouched sector was that of florists in the country. What most people would view as challenges or hurdles appeared as motivation and opportunity to the daring duo.

"It is unorganized, largely untapped and holds a lot of potential for innovation, hence we had the itch to explore a business opportunity here," Sameer rationalizes the reason for their step forward. "Giving and receiving flowers should be a different and beautiful experience. The idea is to make the moment special, relevant and to convey the sentiments the flowers are meant to convey."

With no other organized enterprise catering to this service during the time Sameer and Smriti were conceiving the idea for their enterprise, the concept stood out even before it was implemented. With the idea in place, it was now time to practice their ability to organize this service in a convenient and accessible way that makes the experience extremely appealing for the customers. With an arrangement for Sameer to primarily look after the enterprise and for Smriti to support him while still keeping her software job, in 2004 their brain-child was born by the name of Florista.

However, in three years, Sameer realized that it was a full time responsibility and he could not give up his advertising business to run Florista. He was almost convinced about shutting down the business, as along with the initial success, a whole lot of challenges had also cropped up. It was at this juncture that Smriti saved the day. She quit her job in 2007 to take Florista on. From then on, the couple has been handling this beautifully crafted partnership together in symbiosis with each other's crafts and intelligence as their true support and strength. Sameer controls the branding, communication and innovations for Florista, and Smriti manages the entire operations, and business development franchising.

From a phase of uncertainties to undecided progress, they have evolved into a stable and flourishing enterprise with a running call centre in Mumbai, training and delivery workshop for artists, and as many as fifteen franchised stores in nine cities across India, and one store in Bhutan. Boosting their creative input into the venture, the duo has poured in all their resources showing everyone how important Florista is for them. This is strongly reflected in both big things and small, to show how family-like the enterprise has become for the duo. Sameer's advertising agency has been his first love and was named Bridge Communications after their son Brij.

"When we were thinking of names for the floral business, we were looking at something connected with our daughter's name Teesta, so flowers combined with Teesta became Florista. It coincidentally happened to be a Spanish word for 'flower girl' and that's how we started visualizing it. For us, Florista became like our baby girl who we dearly love and care about," expresses Smriti with a strong tone of conviction.

Not only have they managed to tap an unexplored industry and make a flourishing enterprise out of it, but have also succeeded in realizing their dreams and pursuing their passion and education to their hearts' content. Having different interests and passions has turned out to be a blessing for them as well as the venture. Sameer ensures that customer communication is perfect. From shop manager to artist to delivery boy, everybody projects a consistently positive image of the brand. Possessing both experience as well as deep understanding of the advertising and marketing framework for an organization, he takes the reins of the creative aspect from finalizing the name of the brand to its imagery.

"All seasonal creatives (posters, danglers, emailers) are conceptualized in-house by Sameer and his agency and I have to say without being biased that they do an incredible job," Smriti speaks fondly.

She herself has brought about a completely different element of Florista to light after joining the partnership.

"When Smriti moved in, she brought in an efficient use of technology into the business and extraordinarily handled the development of the e-commerce site, introduced an order management software which helped manage volumes, as well as managed the responsibility of training the team for the use of technology," Sameer speaks in equal admiration of his wife.

The early adoption of technology helped in scaling the business and become a differentiator from competitors then. As one of the best examples of complimentary equations, both of them are bringing to the table their individual skills, experience and perspective, at the same time integrating them into a singular aim and operation. This not only strengthens their entrepreneurial quotient, but also helps them evolve tremendously as a couple, in their personal lives as well.

Despite what may appear to be a thriving enterprise now, Florista and the couple have seen their share of ups and downs. Standing together through all these challenges, the duo has helped each other out in varied circumstances.

"My parents were not very happy. Selling flowers was not exactly a respectable profession, especially for a techie," Smriti makes light of the situation in retrospection.

Over the years, when the brand started getting recognized, a lot of media coverage helped to increase the popularity of the enterprise. This was when Florista began to be recognised as a significant and niche name, convincing a lot of friends and family to finally build faith and appreciation for the couple and their endeavour. Raising funds was not the easiest task.

"Getting the operations to roll out smoothly, ensuring quality to be maintained and to manage payments was a challenge in itself," Sameer reflects on the challenges of the venture. "Also, since flowers are a quickly perishable segment of products, it was essential to ensure that the flow of orders and delivery was in sync with each other and caused minimum loss of resources. That was not as easy as it sounds."

The tipping point was when the florist was gearing up for the next phase of growth and needed investments desperately. At this stage, banks refused to sanction loans because Florista had no assets in the company. However, in 2010, things took an upside when the couple sought the help of some investment bankers. After having put both their houses on mortgage, to be able to secure financial support was a sigh of relief for the two, although it did come with a lot of responsibilities and commitments. Acknowledging this phase as the most trying period of their lives, the two do accept that these were the times when they took some of the boldest and bravest decisions, because they knew they had each other's back. With their conviction, Smriti and Sameer have turned these challenges into prized achievements. Lots of learnings have come in hindsight, as they were still picking up as they grew in scale and experience. Turning back, Smriti wishes they could have gone digital a lot earlier, hence not only saving on a lot of cost but also scaling up considerably on the platform.

Today, with a forty-five member team, Smriti and Sameer holistically concentrate on building a consistent quality of services that differentiates them with a unique identity.

"Training on empathy is crucial; we deal with special occasions and sentiments. It is important for our call centre team to understand that while handling an issue," Sameer speaks about the categorical expectation from his team.

With the business being an integral part of their lives, Sameer and Smriti find themselves immersed in the world of Florista with their heart and soul. While roles and responsibilities are divided and independent decisions are respected between the two of them, sometimes, boundaries are crossed and conflicts arise. Similarly, for the couple, the boundary between home and work has blurred as the two often communicate about official issues at home, especially with family.

"We've had our share of tense scenes, when conflicts move from office desks and enter the walls of our home. So, with experience, we have mutually decided not to discuss points of conflict at home," Smriti speaks in a tone of serious resolution.

Further enhancing the involvement and understanding that the couple has created in their equation, they speak frankly about breaking the myth of not bringing the family into the work arena.

"On the contrary, I have realized that sharing information at home helps tremendously. We discuss with our children certain issues in business and they do in their own way try and give their views on the same. It has helped them understand appreciate why we keep long hours away from home," Smriti speaks with a sense of satisfaction.

In complete sync with the sentiments of their business, the duo firmly believes that flowers bring people together. They appreciate the fact that with Florista, they too have grown and matured in their relationship with each other.

"It was like getting married again and learning about each other's skills and improvement areas. We have had our share of disagreements, fights over small issues, but today, we have found our peace," she continues. Making the best of their times, either together or away from each other, the couple spends a good deal of time in their individual zones that helps them evolve their individual aspirations as well. Meeting each other during lunch hours, or when they are travelling together, they usually spend the moments sharing the developments in their respective areas of work. This has become so much a part of their life that often celebrations and other special occasions get entwined with work. "One year, during our anniversary on the 4th of December, we had got a large floral décor order for American Express Bank and for this, our team had to work overnight and one of us needed to be there to supervise the work. All our plans went out of the window. So we decided to celebrate it at the site. We monitored the work, went for a drive around Colaba at around midnight, had a quick dinner at a fancy restaurant and went back to the work site," Smriti recalls with a happy sparkle in her eyes.

Recalling several other times where the two have spent memorable moments, Sameer talks about how stressful times also change into fun when the two are together, "Once we carried the flowers ourselves and delivered it to the people. It was amazing watching the smiles on their faces when the flowers were handed over."

Florista often serves as a cherished and rewarding platform offering very personal and intimate involvement at all levels.

Treating all achievements with gratitude, the two appreciate each other at home and at work, and the duo is a perfect example of appreciating every little achievement that has helped them grow bit by bit.

"There were several moments of pride – our first franchise sign up, first store, first store out of Mumbai, first media coverage, first investment, etc. A celebration for us is taking a quick weekend break away from the city."

Even spending their day with high energy, with the customer service team, paying attention to clients' responses and feedback, giving a lot of time to the accounts and operations and taking reports are activities that the duo enjoy with absolute dedication. While they are aggressively looking forward to expansion plans, they envisage a model of operation by going completely digital in terms of mobile apps, better payment options, etc. Florista is also looking at expanding its product portfolio, getting into wedding event management and franchising the brand outside India. With so much positivity and productivity being generated by Sameer and Smriti, one is bound to see success and satisfaction in their enterprise. While many aspiring entrepreneurs admire this example of success, they look on curiously to see what new heights will this partnership scale.

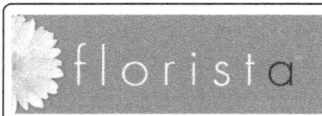

If you have to send flowers and gifts to someone special anywhere across the country, visit www.florista.in or catch them on Facebook at /florista.in.

"Attraction is common. What's rare is having someone who wants to grow & build with you. A soul partner, a soul confidante, a soul mate."

GreenNGood *is the brainchild of* **Aparna & Vinay**, *making available products of everyday use that are made by small scale cottage industries, differently-abled people or artisans. With this holistic and organic approach, they are encouraging value adding purchase habits, also empowering people from weaker segments of the society.*

A Green and Good Business – GREENnGOOD

By Aparna & Vinay

Today's is a fast-paced world of economics where goods are sold and purchased in thousands every second. Amidst the crazy pile of these transactions, there's hardly ever a minute when the buyers stop to think where this seemingly inexhaustible supply of resources is coming from, or what will be the consequences of the use of the mostly artificially-produced, chemical-based products. Similarly, sellers or manufacturers usually do not take the onus of supplying goods in the market with a sense of responsibility with respect to what sources they are coming from, or what consequences they are going to have in the ecological system during and after consumption. This indiscriminate rate of consumption and supply is not reflective of a healthy future in terms of the environmental, economic or even social well-being, and if the process is not checked today, a ghastly future, seen in films or told in stories will become an inevitable reality. While most of us turn a blind eye towards this important issue and go about our consumerist approach of convenience, there are a very few conscious souls amidst us who are trying to mainstream the concept of responsible consumerism in order to create an awareness and an impact for the larger good. This is the story of one such enterprising endeavour of two people, dedicated in their passion to make a difference.

Aparna knew long before she even got into studying business that someday she wanted to enter mainstream enterprising. However, unlike what most people would have believed, her idea was not to start another brand selling commercial commodities to people amidst the hoard of many such names. On the contrary, her idea was to create a social impact in a way that finds way into the awareness scheme of the conventional audience so that it does not merely remain social work, but takes the form of a large scaled sustainable model of impact. With this intention, the young girl from Jaipur joined one of the most premier business schools of the country in Ahmedabad. There, while education and experience was teaching her the fundamentals of the business world, life were teaching her the real time lessons of understanding people, associations and companionship. And in the process, she met Vinay, who would go on to become one of the most influential and supportive members of her life. The then young man from Andhra Pradesh, with a knack for finance, had also joined the business school with the aim of strengthening his understanding of the commercial aspects of the world. It's no surprise that theirs became a love story seen in the movies – the two coming from different backgrounds, different states, and different cultures. They stood against the odds and soon after completing their post-graduation, tied the holy knot of matrimony to take their companionship a notch higher.

But unlike most love stories that end with a happy wedding, theirs had just about begun.

"It's been like this since the beginning," explains Aparna with fond recollection, "Vinay always understood me, accepted whatever my aspirations were and always went out of his way to support me."

The beginning of their respective careers was more or less conventional. While Vinay moved on to the banking sector to establish himself as an efficient banker, Aparna dabbled in data analysis, microfinance, and most importantly, in the social working sector, that can claim responsibility in giving her a significant push into what would become her passion eventually.

"During my graduation, I used to volunteer with NGOs. Coming in close contact with people who were making methodical impact on the environment, supporting those who suffer or are underprivileged had a deep impact on me," she explains.

Having worked with important issues like women empowerment, environment, rural and tribal lives as well as differently abled people, Aparna went through an inner stimulation that motivated her to work on the lines of making a social impact. What formulated the most significant impression was her experience of working with an organization called Seva Mandir that exposed her to a non-glamorous and deprived segment of the society. It was during the course of her research and step by step discoveries into deeper understanding of the philanthropic actions that she stumbled into the concept of responsible consumerism. Explaining the principle as a "phenomenon which encourages us as consumers to be responsible and aware towards the transactions we are making, in a way to promote products that are resource efficient and sustainable, both for the planet as well as the people."

Thus, with this mantra to drive her, Aparna quit her job in 2008 and went on to build a brand that has today come to be known as GreenNGood. With categorical identification of the problem or what is commonly known as the market opportunity, she recalls her horrid realization with respect to pollution, loss of livelihoods for small scale cottage industries of craftsmen or simply the blatant vanishing of traditional knowledge – all as a result of a capitalist rush of consuming public goods. Labelling these effects as something no one ever pays a price for, she goes on to dissect the undiscerning habit as a mere 'sale' with each transaction, indifferent of the larger hemorrhage it is creating in the eco-system.

Thus, GreenNGood emerged as a hallmark solution that not only aimed to create awareness among people about responsible consumerism, but also provided a direction for actionable solutions with its own range of products being made available, accessible and affordable for people in India through the online portal that is both cost effective and immensely scalable. With over six thousand products that are organic, natural and eco-friendly, GreenNGood caters to a variety of needs of the modern day consumer. From clothing to food, cosmetics to detergents, from home cleaning products to décor, a plethora of goods are manufactured and supplied, keeping in mind environmental standards, which include healthier, safer ingredients, and most of them packed with bio-degradable materials. And to add to that, most of these products are made by people working in small cottage industries. A lot of them employ underprivileged women, differently-abled people or artisans with skills in colloquial art forms. Thus, with a more holistic and organic approach, the venture promotes not only the products, but also consequentially value adding purchase habits that may eventually lead to a healthy and sustainable lifestyle.

"We are in the process of creating a movement here. You buy consciously, in turn you act consciously, talk about it with your peers, family and colleagues too. I am hoping that every single place that a GreenNGood product or packaging travels, it will create a wave of impact," explains the passionate visionary.

Starting out with her savings from her five years in various organizations, a blessed boost for Aparna came when her friend and husband Vinay finally quit his bank job in 2011 and decided to join her full time. Not only was this a symbol of great psychological support for her, but he also brought a new perspective and financial expertise along.

"Vinay had continued with his job to earn enough money for funding, to be able to bootstrap the venture for the time being. His joining us full time was both a relief and absolutely welcome," she reveals.

As someone who had been supportive of her entrepreneurial streak even back in college, Vinay not only understood Aparna's inclinations, but also helped her refine the product lines and range for GnG – a critical decision that helped determine the flow of business eventually. Hence, the couple, complimenting each other with their respective skill sets, bring together an environment which is both fundamentally as well as practically exciting and sustainable, thanks to the exemplary Yin and Yan of the duo.

"While Aparna defines the ethos of our organization and brings creativity to each and every segment, I take care of the operational and financial sections. I guess we can't possibly go wrong with things we feel so passionately about!" exclaims Vinay.

However, what may appear to be a hunky dory picture of perfection today has had its due share of challenges while they were starting out. Like any startup, GreenNGood was not immune to initial apprehensions.

"Quitting mainstream jobs and diving into something which does not have a certainty cushion is a challenge every entrepreneur has to pass through at some stage," Vinay talks about the tough times in retrospection, "especially when you are starting with something offbeat and trying to merge it into a mainstream enterprise. Functioning out of only personal savings, there were tied hands in several areas for the duo and tough decisions had to be made in terms of expenditure.

"If we had had the luxury of funds, we would have been able to invest more diligently in marketing and customer service," he marks in hindsight.

Also, family support was of utmost importance, and that's one essential element that kept them going. "My parents have been the biggest strength for us during entrepreneurship. In fact, we stayed with them at Jaipur while we were starting up. They always believed in us and kept encouraging us throughout, even when times were tough. Our story would be incomplete without mentioning their contribution. My father is a retired Air Force Doctor (Gp.Capt. M.S. Bhatnagar), and Mom (Karuna Bhatnagar) is a home maker and they live in Jaipur where we started GreenNGood.com. They also financially invested in our business to help us start up...they both looked after us like kids studying for an exam so that we had all the time to focus on our work. This was really very helpful in the initial years!" they fondly recollect.

Initiating a business that depended massively on business to business collaboration, bringing so many sources and producers on board with GreenNGood was definitely not a slice of cake.

"To get people on board with an idea that is still under incubation is challenging, especially when it's something they haven't heard or experienced before," says Aparna from experience. There were a lot of things happening for the first time for the couple – the most unpredictable of those being working together as partners. While convention warns against such a partnership, Aparna and Vinay went ahead to face this challenge with the most matured and insightful perspective. Despite the hurdles that have come their way in maintaining and expanding the venture with its objectives intact, the couple has managed to fight through together.

"We have been blessed with a lot of well-wishers – both family and friends who have been extremely supportive," adds Aparna with her gentle smile. Placing her faith and gratitude in her brother who has been a constant force of strength and wisdom, she goes on to take advice from him even today.

Hard work and sincerity have brought the dedicated duo a long way with their endeavours. Amidst the cloud of trepidations, when the business was still in the process of finding a firm footing, came their moment of glory. The Think Big Challenge happened.

"Winning the prestigious challenge was not only a big boost to our morale, but also provided for the seed funding that helped us get better structure and build a better team. In the phase of starting up, this was a huge support, both psychologically as well as financially," Aparna explains with a hint of pride.

Milestones of achievement on the way have been very helpful in bringing a great opportunity to level up. "With accomplishment like making it to the top three at The Pitch, or receiving awards like the Karmaveer Chakra or a fellowship coming your way, you are made to feel that you are doing something right, both technically and ethically!" she exclaims with humility.

Working for what they are passionate about has more incentives than just monetary gains or social recognition. Aparna recognizes the enterprise as being her golden opportunity to interact with a variety of artists, thinkers and activists, who have, in their actions, contributed to responsible citizenship. Not only does GreenNGood allow for her to act upon her ideology of being fundamentally conscious about the eco-system, but also gives her a chance to meet with artisans across the country, and to discover new art forms and traditional methods.

The business that has been created out of this opportunity simply holds on the basis of transparent and effective partnership with manufacturers linked with small cottage industries, with traditional and colloquial artists and with creators belonging to the marginalized segments of the society. The model works on a simple per sale commission basis that GreenNGood earns for every product purchased through its outlet which is designed online.

"This not only helps to create a platform where artists and producers can find visibility and scale, but also helps formulate a strategy that is consciously sustainable, both ecologically and economically," Vinay adds insightfully.

With a small yet effective family of five members that forms the team, GreenNGood has been consistent with its growth and partnerships. The team works with one common objective and integrity. For this, they are carefully selected as members who feel passionately about the environment and the cause, and are willing to break boundaries and take ownership. Breaking through the trend of environment friendly not being accepted because of their cost, Aparna believes and propagates the philosophy that it is far cheaper to pay in cash than to exhaust every possible resource of the planet till a point of no return.

As a couple who spend a lot of their time together, one might wonder how they find their work-home balance. Despite being assumed as a challenging equation, Aparna and Vinay seem to have cracked the mystery code with regards to the respect and understanding they have for each other. Keeping individual egos aside, they work together in bringing success and contentment, both in their personal and professional life.

"The idea is to respect each other's space and decisions. This shows complete faith and understanding. This is what keeps us balanced," Vinay says insightfully. Each believes in spending as much time on his or her own as they do with each other and maintain a healthy atmosphere by keeping physically fit, spiritually aligned and socially balanced. With gratitude and understanding as the driving force of everything they have received, it feels only symbolic that the partners are committed to a cause so serene in its objective.

Unlike most enterprising people, this duo does not believe in aggressive ambitions. Unhealthy desires driven with the motivation of money and power has already brought a stack full of businesses to their current state today, with indiscriminate and unthoughtful cycles of demand and supply.

"While we do believe in expansion, we understand that it has to be organic and natural, not merely competitive and commercial. Hence, GreenNGood works towards holistic growth with each step rather than mere economic development," Aparna thoughtfully reveals the ethos of what drives the venture ahead.

While every competition is not worth feeling insecure about, she does acknowledge its importance as it helps the organization remain on their toes and continue to strive for excellence. With such powerful principles, Aparna and Vinay are glistening ahead with a phenomenon that reflects not only on their strength in principle, but also goes on to talk mightily about the movement it is headed to create towards responsible consumerism. As an example set in the country for many to learn and draw from, they have managed to create an environment, both in their work, as well as in life that radiates positive and influential energy that has immense potential of affecting the larger cosmos of life.

Disha & Ravi *found* **Imagimake** *to make learning fun for children, as against the boring mugging up culture that seemed to be catching up fast. In researching and coming up with innovative games and attractive puzzles, they have changed the way the country wishes to educate its next generations.*

Playtime at Work – IMAGIMAKE

By Disha & Ravi

Who says professional and personal lives do not or should not intersect? The old myth has long been busted and people have begun to realize that some of the best decisions at the professional front have a personal influence; and being professional with personal aspirations, on the other hand, is often the key to accomplish a lot of dreams. Contrary to common belief and fear, the definition of words like work and career only need to be looked at with a fresh perspective to understand that the phenomenon goes beyond a conventional nine to five schedule, beyond salary accounts and beyond resume transfers from one organization to the next.

In this new age growth of extremely skilled and creative 'professionals', one notices a change in the value system, in opportunities and in the fast rising enterprising spirit of the people. This is the era of startups. A whole new school of thought that believes in building something unique and independent is sparking in today's generation, and while on the one hand some entrepreneurs are willing to explore some of the most innovative and precarious ideas that have never been explored as business propositions, others are bringing their own twist of creativity in the pre-existing business opportunities, customizing and modernizing platforms that were fast depleting into archaic models, converting them into extremely attractive and lucrative enterprises, and carving a niche for themselves in the market.

Most of the stories about such entrepreneurs remain hidden from public eyes as we are on the receiving end of only the services. However, when such examples come to light, not only do they make us understand the mechanism that goes behind the scene, but also inspires us to dream big and realize that the journey is both enriching and promising. One such journey that comes to mind is that of Disha and Ravi.

As a couple who were once as conventionally professional as it gets, their leap in life has been a drastic one. Hailing from academically strong backgrounds, the duo has created an interesting blend of their education and work experience. Disha comes with a degree in mathematics and operation research with a post-graduation in business management. Ravi, on the other hand, has his degree in production engineering and post-graduation in business management. They happened to cross paths while working in the same organization – one of the most reputed firms in the world.

"The organization was a big one and the chances that you don't even stumble into a lot of your colleagues are pretty high. But when you have it in your destiny, you will meet your soulmate one way or another!" Ravi exclaims with a sense of awe.

It is said that if you really want to find out whether you love or hate someone, you should start working with them. Thankfully, for this couple, it sprouted into the former. Having been placed together for a few projects, the two worked with each other in an ambience of tight deadlines and high pressure expectations. However, in this critical tug of war, where most people experience fall-outs with even their closest friends, Ravi and Disha found themselves drawing closer to each other. As events fell into place one after another, the couple got together and finally tied the nuptial knot in 2011. While most stories would end with this happily ever after, for these two, it had only just begun!

As two ambitious people who believe in a continuous growth process, Ravi and Disha soon started exploring further options in life. In the meantime, Ravi switched his job to handle operations of an entire zone for one of the biggest names in India. Whether it was a change in environment, a new light of perspective or simply the entrepreneurial bug that bit the two, but the events that followed changed everything about them – from being an ordinary married couple to becoming partners in a different journey.

"I think it began as an idea inspired from day to day life. Whenever we would visit our friends or family who had kids, it was a common observation that the children lacked a holistic mechanism to play and learn, to create or be expressive in their age-appropriate activities. This was either due to lack of resources or due to lack of time from the parents' front," Disha recalls. This got the couple thinking and thus began a deliberate phase of brain storming to explore this gap as an opportunity for setting up a creative venture.

Never the sorts to let things be, the husband and wife pursued this idea till the end, and thus, in 2012, they decided to start off with Imagimake, an innovative platform dedicated to help children express themselves creatively. Based out of Mumbai, this became an activity centre and a retail outlet with an aim to deliver some of the most creative and formative experiences in the lives of children. The idea was to make available some extremely creative games and projects, and to provide an environment within the centre where children could find assistance in expressing themselves through these innovative models.

"Within six months of starting Imagimake, we had a customer base of about five hundred kids from the locality," Disha explains with pride. "Soon we started getting lot of enquiries from all over Mumbai to conduct workshops, birthday parties and playdates for children, and we gradually expanded our team to include event specialists and child trainers. The concept of having a creative birthday party wherein children work together to create a nice takeaway for themselves was an instant hit!"

Taking this journey forward, the enterprising couple delved deeper into the opportunity and found out that many games and play tools available for children are generic, repetitive, inferior in quality or too expensive. This then encouraged the creative think tanks to build their own line of products for children.

Describing the unique selling point of the venture, Ravi explains, "The idea was to create a range which actually serves the true purpose of Imagimake – that it had to be innovative, easy, affordable and have a higher play value. No other product line offers this quality with accessibility in the country like us!"

As a perfect example of a venture that does not satiate its growth with a single sail of success, Imagimake, through consistent endeavours of Ravi and Disha, has come up with further innovations. Labelling only the sky as their limit, Ravi admits that there is no decided limiting target, but Imagimake wants to continue evolving on its path with bigger and better innovations.

"We didn't have any limiting criteria for any specific genre of toys in mind to begin with, and firmly believe in continually exploring different ideas in art and craft, puzzles, model making and board games. Over a period of time, we have moved from creating individual units to an innovative play system which provides the right set of tools, materials and guidance to the kids and helps them explore their own creativity. This is where Quill On was born. Quill On is a creative play system based on the art of paper quilling with the patent pending Super Quiller being at its core. Within the first year, it has reached more than twenty thousand happy customers and made its way into the curriculum of reputed schools in Mumbai."

Having worked hard, both on the front of product innovation, as well as its marketing strategies, the co-founders have brought Imagimake to a level of accomplishment today that most entrepreneurs find hard to imagine. Since the very launch, the brand has not only found its identity despite being an out of the mill idea, but also been accepted widely, spreading its good reputation across different platforms. With a reach across more than twenty prominent cities across the country, Imagimake finds presence in some of the most prestigious outlets. For a product range that has come up with an innovative aim and idea, Imagimake seems to be doing very well, with over a hundred thousand items sold only in the previous year! It is not only a mark of success for the ambitious entrepreneurs, but also an important source of motivation for the entire organization to continue their striving for excellence.

Having proved their quality and innovation unswervingly, Ravi and Disha continue to study and research diligently for better possibilities. In all their humility, they never boast of the appreciable zenith they have climbed, but it is a well published fact that ever since the launch of their extraordinary line of products, the co-founders have been bagging some of the most prestigious awards of the country. Ask them what it feels like to have so many feathers to their cap and you get a gentle smile.

"It is very motivating and humbling that we have been loved and accepted, and are somewhere on the right track with our mission in helping children create and express themselves freely," says Disha.

Building Imagimake step by step has been a full time passion for this power-house bustling with energy. From observation to execution to aggressive expansion, the perfect combination of Ravi and Disha has seen the organization rise to its current strength. Currently functioning with the strength of forty-five people in the team, Imagimake boasts of some of the most efficient professionals working across design, operations, sales and marketing. While career growth in this excessively innovative and competitive enterprise is motivation enough for all the team members, it is largely the vision, synchronized with every new person coming on board that gets the Imagimake family excited about a dedicated performance. As a unit that celebrates all its success and learnings (they refuse to believe in failures) from the smallest ideas to the biggest awards, it is a delight to see this work place bustling with synergy, creativity and perfection.

From the beginning till the end, one can witness the commitment at all levels. From brainstorming sessions, to attentive detailing of sales, from strategic analysis of marketing techniques to staying connected with the latest developments in the market environment, all activities become a part of the team's daily life. It is not hard to identify the source of such a temperament. With both the co-founders exhibiting unexhausted reserves of dedication, all the verticals of the enterprise find their due share of attention. While Disha takes it upon her shoulders to go out of her way to organize and facilitate the proceedings of the day, Ravi, on the other hand, is naturally a people's person and finds it immensely necessary to create an environment that is conducive to productivity.

Speaking of Ravi and Disha at work together, their natural compatibility clicks is the most obvious first impression one gets. As complementary pillars of cooperation and understanding, the co-founders have an equal share of roles and responsibilities in the enterprise that accentuates their own skills and experiences, bringing out the best of this partnership. With her expertise, Disha handles the product design, development and go-to market for new launches, thus taking care of all the backstage responsibilities. Ravi takes over the baton when the product is launched to drive sales, fulfillment and revenue generation for Imagimake. Efficiently, with their mutual cooperation, they complete the cycle. As co-founders, they enjoy the rights and roles with respect to each other's opinions too, setting an example for everyone to follow. "There are of course differences that pop up between us. But since we both sincerely mean what is best for the company, these differences are also taken in good spirit, and we try coming to a conclusion that is most suitable," Ravi puts it wisely.

As two people who have seen each other through the thick and thin of life so far, both Disha and Ravi unanimously acknowledge each other's support as the proud reason of their collective success. From having to bootstrap for all expenses, making the critical decisions of quitting mainstream lucrative jobs, to every stage of the expansion that comes with its share of risks, the two have stood tall in each other's support. The challenges have been in plenty, and the lack of entrepreneurial experience also came with its share of conflicts. However, at the fundamental level, the couple has been strong and certain of their ambition and methodical in their pursuit.

"The key has been trust. I know I can count on him, no matter what. I am not dependent on any external person who is bound to have principle conflicts or ego clashes with me. For us, it's a passion," Disha expresses candidly.

Dismissing the presumption of work and home boundaries as a cause of turmoil in one's personal life, she explains that when something as personal and passionate as this becomes one's work, there is no scope of differentiating what is personal or professional. In all fairness, one can simply observe that this professional pursuit of the duo has also helped them evolve tremendously in the personal zone as well. Both as individuals and partners, with each other's support and respect, they always find new sources of motivation and celebration. If you're wondering what are the odds of such passion ending up into something inconsequential, it does not worry this couple.

"If it were not Imagimake, I am sure we would have been creating magic somewhere else. I refuse to believe that with our belief and passion, we would fail. It is just that the journey has chances of both hills and valleys, depends on how you perceive it," Ravi concludes with a smile of satisfaction. Grabbing his bag, he wraps up for the day and heads out for a waiting Disha at the door. Their chitter-chatter seems like any ordinary couple, revolving around each other and their own dreams and hopes. They walk away to embrace the closing of another satisfactory day of their life, leaving behind lingering thoughts of a tale that lives to inspire many others to chase their dreams with similar enthusiasm.

| **Imagi make** | If you also wish to make learning fun for kids around you, do visit www.imagimake.com or follow them on Facebook at /Imagimake. |

Having struggled to find a platform in India that enabled business owners to exit from their set-up with gains, **Bhavin & Priya** *set up* **Indiabizforsale.com** *that lists businesses on sale and connects sellers with prospect buyers.*

An Enterprising Affair – INDIABIZFORSALE

By Bhavin & Priya

In a fast rising and highly innovative space of startups in the Indian business world, there is hardly any dimension of enterprise that has not been explored and experimented with. Aspiring entrepreneurs with the best of experience and skills, education and passion have tried their hands at almost all the verticals from food to fashion, health to housing. However, with best of the minds dedicated into exploring the most unique enterprises that hold potential of becoming phenomenal business opportunities, even the sky is not the limit. To tap on an opportunity which has not yet been established as a safe and secured business idea, and yet make a thirst in the market for such a platform, raising it from ground zero into an exemplary enterprise, would be desirable. It is one thing to hail from a background that is embedded in business and pick up from such a privilege to build something of your own, and entirely another thing to give up on the comfort and luxury of an extremely lucrative and stable career to start something from scratch and make a ruling enterprise out of it. Very rare examples of such passion and hard work come to light, but when they do, they create a story worth learning from.

The lead characters of our story are two scholars who have dedicated their passion and knowledge of business development towards preparing an organized platform that can benefit many in this country. Priya has earned her Master's degree in international finance and is a member of the Association of Chartered Certified Accountants (ACCA). After completing her Master's degree in commerce, she moved to UK with an aim of gaining an in-depth knowledge of the subject. Bhavin, on the other hand, holds a Bachelor's degree in chemistry, with a deep knowledge in the pharma sector. Post his studies in India, he too went to the UK to pursue a post-graduation degree in management. It was a stroke of luck that got them face to face with each other in very unlikely circumstances. In the process of pursuing their post-graduation, both Priya and Bhavin were looking for part time jobs. The duo landed up with part time jobs at the same place. Their first introduction as colleagues easily graduated into a warm friendship. Having found a lot of common interests, the two were often found socializing with each other. It was not hard to forecast the budding relationship that soon sprouted between the two. Sharing a relatable background of experience, passion for business and commerce, and finding a deep felt love and faith in each other, Bhavin and Priya finally decided to get married after a courtship of about four years. Since both their families are rooted in India, the couple went back home for a beautiful wedding ceremony, after which, they returned to England to pursue their respective careers. However, what fate held for them was designed in a way far more intense and expanded than a simple couple leading a predictable life.

It is often said that the best teacher comes in the form of experience, and the ones to learn the lessons in this process are the wisest ones. This wise couple also made the best of their experiences and challenges and made something unique out of it!

"In 2010, one of our family businesses had some management issues and they were looking to exit from the business. We used traditional methods of print advertisement in newspapers and ended up spending a considerable amount of money for the advertisements. We also appointed some business brokers to work out the best deal for us, but after a few months and a lot of resource investment, we realized that all our efforts were going in vain and we lost a disproportionate amount of time and money doing it," recalls Bhavin, delving into what triggered the genesis of this venture. Having seen this challenge, Bhavin and Priya had already started directing their resources using global online platform for business, and managed to generate more than sixty inquiries for the business from all over the world. With this personally enlightening experience, the duo, with their inherent talent, immediately recognized a business opportunity that could be immediately addressed to create a successful enterprise.

"That time, no platform was focusing with any serious planning or resources to provide services in India that would cater to support the buying or selling of a business," Priya recollects. "Whilst sitting in the UK, the series of events got us wondering about what really happens to the small and medium sized companies in India, when the owner wants to exit the business."

This contemplation led to a lot of extensive research on the matter, which consequently brought to them the idea that even though there were many successfully established models to facilitate the buying and selling of businesses around the world, there was not such an organized facility available in their homeland. In the summer of 2012, the couple decided to take a nosedive into this idea and build something around this while they were still in the UK. With their aim focused on creating a solution for the problems faced by business owners who wanted to sell their businesses as an exit, their endless brainstorming and calculation resulted in formulating a simple, effective online platform to buy and sell businesses in India.

"We took time out of work for this whilst doing our full-time jobs and worked hard to put together a business model. Thus, amidst the nerve-straining schedule managing their professional careers and a budding new enterprise, catering to the Indian market while residing in a foreign land, was born www.indiabizforsale.com in January 2013.

"It is basically SMEs' Discovery Platform for M&A, Investment Opportunities and Business Partnerships in India. The platform is specifically focused on the Indian market. The name itself tells you what the business does; i.e. Business for Sale in India," Bhavin puts it crisply.

Although they had launched a functional website with basic details in the hope of creating a buzz about Indiabizforsale, the couple soon realized that it wasn't going to be as easy as they had imagined. Putting together the business model was only the tip of the iceberg of their hard work, and the real challenge actually lay in bringing the businessmen in India to the awareness of such a service.

"It seemed as if people were not even aware that you could sell your business or even buy one for expansion!" exclaims Priya.

However, having realized the real face of their challenge, the dynamic entrepreneurs immediately got into a solution mode and decided to the hit the nail on the head. Their effective solution to the problem of spreading the word came in the form of a tool which has fast been gaining popularity; they decided to turn to social media.

"No one can deny the role social media plays in setting up business trends and putting ideas in people's brains. We started writing articles and blogs, sending newsletters to target audience on guiding and educating the entrepreneurs and started building our visibility," she explains about the strategic intervention that was crucial to the initial kick start of the enterprise.

Apart from the issue of creating awareness, the initiation of the business also came with a lot of other challenges. Although the idea had been conceived and introduced in the UK, the couple soon realized that for actual hands on implementation, they would need to build direct relationships with networks in the country. This meant moving back to India and starting from scratch!

"That decision wasn't easy," Bhavin expresses candidly. "We both had lucrative jobs, the cushion of our comfortable lifestyle, our friends and associates, and a vast network we had both gained individually with years of experience in the UK."

However, it was partly the commitment towards Indiabizforsale and partly their unconditional belief and support for each other that encouraged them to take this leap of faith, move back to India and start working on ground zero. This decision was met with both happiness and anxiety. Even back at home, as the couple jointly recollects, while their families were extremely happy to have their children return to India after many years of living away from them, the apprehension of leaving their lucrative careers out of nowhere and diving into unknown waters was a matter of concern. However, the credibility of these skilled professionals, along with their dedicated commitment towards carving their own niche in the Indian market, gave them the support to camp Indiabizforsale on Indian grounds. Without the facility or luxury of any external funding, the duo bootstrapped and put all their savings at stake with complete faith in their enterprise.

What would have appeared to be scarier than anything else to ordinary people was interpreted as challenging and exciting by this extraordinary couple. With education, experience and a lot of conviction to their credit, the two co-founders plunged in with minimum entrepreneurial experience, so to speak, and yet managed to set up a venture that was ground-breaking even from its initial days. Between the couple, they split the roles and responsibilities on the basis of both their interests and abilities. Prior to assuming the company's leadership, Priya had spent more than ten years in the UK and brings over eight years of finance and accounting experience from diverse industry segments, having worked for some of the business giants that exist, gaining expertise in several roles. With such a valued expertise, she now oversees Finance, Operations and IT in the enterprise. Bhavin, on the other hand, brings over fourteen years of experience in business development, sales and marketing. He works closely with the core business development team executing strategic initiatives.

"His robust business acumen has a proven track record in building and developing businesses, managing client relations and ensuring business profitability, and it is an absolute delight to partner up with him at the work front. And I am not just saying this because he is my husband!"Priya speaks with adoration.

With each other's hand as their strongest support system, the two have managed to turn Indiabizforsale into one of the leading enterprises in their domain.

"From the idea to its inception and launching the full version of the website, to achieving the first milestone of four hundred businesses for sale listings that has now grown to eight hundred plus sell-side listings and thirteen hundred plus buy-side listings, we sure have come a long way!" Bhavin gleams with a sense of well-earned pride. Recounting every little achievement that has come their way and has added critical advantage to their business growth, he also talks about various accomplishments like press coverage by some of the leading media houses of the country, and being chosen to exhibit at some of the most prestigious events in the country, that has helped to surge the glamour quotient and has been extremely effective in pushing the venture in both the national as well international line of vision.

With humility and maturity, the couple believes in offering credit where it is due. With a dedicated family of nine members as a part of their team, they feel proud of working with some of the best employees in their enterprise who function marvelously in the areas of finance, management, sales, marketing, HR, design, customer service and technology. They also do not shy away from acknowledging the support and faith their families have shown in this precarious journey, that has not only helped them go ahead and take bold decisions, but also come closer and stronger as a family.

As a couple that has practically no boundaries between home and work, one might wonder how this equation works out, especially at a personal level. Bhavin and Priya seemed to have mastered the art of Zen and seem to find contentment in the direction they are headed.

"I know it appears like there must be no end to work, or no time for family, but that is hardly the case for us," Priya explains, contrary to expectation. "Our dinners become celebrations, or chocolate sharing with our four-year-old bundle of joy becomes reward for hard work. We are blessed to be able to do what we love and love what we do; hence work is never an external pressure."

Her assurance reflects strongly in the visibly affectionate relationship that the two share, both in their professional as well as personal space. From paying attention to details at work, to getting involved with their team in all big and small accomplishments, from taking out time to connect with each other regarding latest developments, to spacing hours in their personal life to look after each other and their family – this couple seems to have figured out the chemistry just right!

With categorical plans of action and clearly defined roles and responsibilities, one may expect that each day for the two entrepreneurs ticks by the clock. However, it might be surprising to see how accommodating and flexible they can be around each other.

"I think what helps the most is to know how well we understand each other. It is not like there are no conflicts or differences of opinion. But a mutual respect is so deeply embedded in our equation that despite our individual perspectives, we always make way for each other," Priya reveals with serenity. In this current year, the aim is towards aggressive growth, both in terms of scale and intensity of reach, and the duo is set to expand to most key areas in India. With a robust product mix in place and now external funding in hand, there is clearly no stopping thier dynamic march.

If you ask them about their relationship with this enterprise, the content smiles on their faces provides a more revealing answer than any words would. Not only do they narrate their experience as enriching and satisfying, the couple feels no hesitation in expressing what it has done to strengthen their own relationship with each other. Having been each other's support system through the most trying times, they believe that their leap of faith has been the best decision of their lives. As examples of a successful entrepreneurship and relationship as well, they highly recommend aspiring entrepreneurs to work with their life partners to experience the depth of this beautiful equation – one that provides confidence, trust and support, and enriches both, professionally and personally.

*Backed by experience in technology and computer science, **Siddharth & Meena** got together to amalgamate their knowledge, experience and market needs and created **iView Labs**, that is dedicated to delivering customized solutions for information technology.*

Interesting Innovation – iVIEW LABS

By Siddharth & Meena

Sometimes it is a matter of luck that brings two people together. But more often, it's the choices that people make that really get them together in their journey of life. Whether it is about living together, sharing interests, taking important decisions or working together, some people just find their way into each other's lives and make home with faith, love and companionship. When relationships are built on the principles of such heartfelt understanding and companionship, it is natural that a bond is formed in such a way that it alters their personal lives and radiates into the external world. This is the story of one such couple with extraordinary dreams who met by chance and went on to build their individual lives, intertwining their dreams and passions with each other's, and creating something beautiful and productive as a result of such a holistic union.

Siddharth is an engineer who completed his Master's degree in business administration from Boston. For a considerable amount of time, he has worked with wealth management companies in Ahmedabad and holds a strong interest in economics. Even while working as a mainstream professional, he always dreamed about becoming an entrepreneur and starting something of his own. Meena holds a Bachelor's degree in computer science from Mumbai and is passionate about technology innovation. At a common family gathering, the two met and there followed an instant liking for each other. This chanced arrangement led into a nuptial communion of a love in an arranged marriage which brought the two together. Hence, fate got Meena to quit her job in Mumbai and move to Ahmedabad to live with her husband. This turned out to be a much welcomed move for Meena, who had been eager to take a break from her full-time job and explore something new and creative. When the lives of the two seemingly different people connected, they got involved and evolved with each other's interests and ideas.

"In the initial days of our marriage, we used to share stories of our professional experiences and talk about different ideas and products that could be used for a startup. I think that's how we started exploring one of the founding thoughts for our venture," explains Siddharth in retrospection. While the couple was certain that they wanted to break away from the conventional professional life, it was Meena's ultimate idea and push that got the duo to step up, quit their jobs and eventually pursue their collective passion of taking technological innovation to the next level. This led to the foundation of their enterprise, iView Labs that came into form in September 2012.

With a background in technology and computer science, and a history of family business to their credit, the couple created an amalgamation of their knowledge, experience and market needs to develop an enterprise that is dedicated to delivering customized solutions for information technology. Claiming to be the backbone of product companies, they first started out with multi-touch solutions that cater to both hardware and software.

"So basically, a company comes to us with an idea in their head and it becomes our purpose to brainstorm and turn that idea into reality, as far as it is practically possible. Providing personalized solutions is our unique selling point," Meena explains, defining the organizational identity. Speaking of the objective with a stress on innovative solutions, she continues to explain the advent of the brand name with their interest in interaction, innovation and information, hence the word 'I' and with a common objective or view that the couple is exploring, creating a space for research and creative innovation, hence the term labs attached to it. This cumulating of a vision focused on tech-based origination thus came to be known as iView Labs.

With a long term purview of an IT company, the duo pitches the organization as being a dependable source for any business in their tech side of the product or service.

"Whenever we take on a project, we completely internalize the organization and take it as an internal mission to accomplish the task, like it is our own business. We are thus promoting entrepreneurship and ownership as an inherent part of our work culture," Siddharth reveals. With the principle of productizing every solution that they make, iViewLabs ensures that the product remains reusable as a solution. With intelligence and lean solutions as their expertise, the brand has made a gamut of products in the last three years of their actualization. Speaking of the diversity of their service, Meena talks about consciously deciding not to limit the venture within any particular vertical of services.

"We have worked in the field of hospitals, retail, health care, pharmaceuticals and so on, and we constantly strive to improve our experience and extent of service. In the sea of technology, there's never really an end point, so we don't want to stop at any particular benchmark." Epitomizing the intent of innovation in

IT services, iView Labs is an ideal brainchild of innovation and entrepreneurship, born out of a perfect combination of the couple's endearing consistency and creativity.

As two people who stand together with their individual strengths and experiences, both Siddharth and Meena bring to the table their diverse expertise. With a passion for technological generation, Meena revolves her work around tech conception and designing all the innovative solutions with her team. Siddharth, on the contrary, is more of a people's person, who dedicates his experience in working on strategies, connecting with people and connecting them with technology. Thus, the duo makes an interesting combination of quality product and efficient marketing. So, while making sure that the service is both relevant and efficient, they are also ensuring that the product is reaching its client appropriately, in turn creating a cyclic channel of acceptance and sustainable growth, both for the clients as well as for iView Labs.

However, though the story of this entrepreneurial journey seems smooth and enticing, it cannot be denied that the perfect picture has come with its share of initial glitches. Especially in the Indian set up of professional growth, where starting an enterprise is not seen with most encouraging eyes, for Siddharth and Meena to leave their conventional job paths was not an easy decision. Even their parents found it a little hard to digest. However, it only took them a witness of their actual work and the impact it was creating to build their faith and come out with full support for the startup. Convincing the family was not even close to the herculean task of bringing outsiders, both employees and clients, to come on board with iView Labs.

"We were initially operating out of a chamber in my dad's clinic, which was just about large to fit three people. Finding quality people within a startup budget was not easy, especially in a city like Ahmadabad, where startups were not a popular trend then," Siddharth reflects on the initial challenges.

Setting up the team or bringing clients on board with innovative technology was all a matter of building faith, and that did not come by magic right from day one. As a start up, there obviously was a money crunch that limited their investments.

"We could have spent more on research and development, client acquisition and team building, but we did not have that financial liberty," Meena speaks with a sense that reveals struggle and strength all at once. Nonetheless, the duo is extremely proud of the challenges they have overcome with each other. Their companionship, gratitude and dedication towards each other and the company is more than symbolic of their success.

Attributing all the success to the team that has stood strong from the start with their faith and contributions, Siddharth humbly calls himself a mere part of the larger picture. Equally graced with humility is Meena who dedicates her entire attention to evolving the product quality each day and attributes the accomplishments to her partner. A perfect blend of compatibility and dedication, the couple has created a similar environment even at the work place, where individual strengths of each team member is recognized and celebrated, and yet a balanced, holistic respect for mutual decisions is maintained. A strong team of sixteen members now, iView Labs dedicates a lot of time in empowering its employees in quality and strength. In fact, their recruitment process lays great emphasis on the cultural fit of the candidate to understand the emotional compatibility of the seeking member.

"We don't just focus on the numbers on their CV or resume; we thoroughly evaluate their passion, strengths and willingness to do something different each day. We only focus on strengths," Siddharth speaks with insight reflecting on what makes iView

Labs stand out. Even between the two of them, Meena and Siddharth have split their verticals in sync with their skills and strengths. While Meena leads research, product development and execution, Siddharth takes care of sales, finance and operations. While maintaining their individual identities and distinguished strategies, the dedicated duo strives to maintain the equilibrium of the partnership through constant support and respect for each other's space and decisions. It is on the grounds of a common vision and alignment of principles that the two succeed in bringing their individual goals to orient with the common objective, marking a fundamental secret for success in a professional partnership.

Behind this benchmark of entrepreneurial companionship lies a relationship deeply engrained with trust, understanding and complete acceptance of each other's strengths and weaknesses. Just like their professional equation, Meena and Siddharth share an equally compatible and successful relationship in their personal life too.

"When you are starting up, you want people with complementary skills; people who can understand you and people you can trust blindly and entirely. Once you have that, everything else falls into place, because you know that someone has your back!" Meena talks about her equation with Siddharth. "It is the same for us even at home. He knows I am there for him, come what may, and so I am for him. This very fact helps us resolve a lot of seemingly difficult issues with relative ease."

When partners in life become partners at work too, it's natural to lose the work-home boundaries, consciously or otherwise. This sometimes leads to differences of opinions stretching beyond one way or the other. This enterprising couple is not an exception to this phenomenon. However, with maturity and wisdom, they have also learnt to give priority and respect to each other's space.

"It's mostly our little daughter who helps us resolve the issues. Once she is in front of us, work goes off the shelf and what remains is a simple, happy family," Meena breaks down the reason of their happiness with this basic mantra.

Celebrating themselves just as much as they celebrate each other is also a secret that Meena and Siddharth reveal. Finding contentment and happiness in the little milestones that they have achieved together is worth more than any treasure for the duo. Whether it was the moment of acquiring their first clients, making their first successful product or the manifold expansion that has brought them respect and recognition, they have stood by each other and proved to be a constant source of inspiration. Just as in good times, the couple stands with equal strength in tough times too. Speaking of the fast-spreading trend of many people offering tech solutions, they acknowledge the increase in competition level in their sector. But their grace and confidence remains untouched. "It's great to see so many people rising up in our industry; it's both inspiring and challenging. This also helps us to keep a healthy greed for doing something better each time we find that someone has been doing something good. So it's an evolutionary cycle," says Siddharth.

Describing their experience of working with each other as destiny's most beautiful gift, Meena and Siddharth are often seen sitting together, ideating, contemplating and brainstorming about something that the duo have struck a storm with. With their mutual admiration and respect, they have stood out to be an example for many aspiring couples who find faith and compatibility in each other. Breaking away from the myth that personal relationships get ruined in a professional environment, the couple declare in their actions that with such unconditional trust and understanding, relationships only penetrate stronger and deeper, affecting not only each other, but also often creating something extraordinary in the bigger picture.

Speaking with heartfelt experience, they advise rising entrepreneurs to embrace their relations, open up to communication and go with the natural flow of mutual acceptance, rather than trying too hard to prove a point. While iView Labs has gone on to innovate and increase a creative quotient in the field of information technology, Meena and Siddarth have directly or indirectly influenced several people to embrace newer ideas and actions and to explore what they love the most with passion and dedication.

iView

Not limited to any particular vertical of service, iView Labs provides a host of customized solutions for IT. You can contact them on www.iviewlabs.com for more details.

"The healthiest relationships are those where you're a team;
where you protect each other and stand up for one another."
— Sharon Rivkin

Pramod & Rohini *were both inspired to do something meaningful in the realm of alternate learning, by using simple ways like board games and puzzles, that could interest the children and yet educate them more effectively. That's how* **Kitki** *was conceptualized, which now provides several solutions to learning, the fun way.*

Changing the Game of Life – KITKI

By Pramod & Rohini

Some things are bound to happen in a certain way. We might see them as conscious decisions or deliberate actions that we may believe to have taken on our own, but more often than not, one close reflection on the past makes it crystal clear that most of our life-changing events are actually carefully determined strokes of destiny. And no matter how difficult we might assume the challenges to be, they are designed to turn out perfectly fine in the end. When such instances or lives come to light, they project themselves as ideal examples for us to follow the most natural course of our instincts. Two people that met by a chance not only realized they were destined to be together, but also discovered new and exciting aspects of their relationship with each other. They realized that there is much more to a partnership than spending a lifetime together.

When young Rohini was still a student in one of the most premium institutes of the country, it was her passion to contribute to her field of knowledge and thus she joined the economics and finance association of the institution. As a person looking for intellectual growth with an inherent attraction to aesthetics of every element of life, she availed every opportunity in her path to contribute and in turn gain experience with the several occasions falling in her lap as a part of the association. However, the most significant moment happened when she met Pramod in the process of organizing an event for her college festival. Pramod, her senior from college, was the secretary of the association back then, and together, with their management and creative skills, they worked on the event.

"I was leading most of the admin work, while Rohini took care of making everything look absolutely pretty. Ten years later, we are still doing the same," reflects Pramod amalgamating the sentiments of the past and the present. The couple spent their college years complementing each other's skills and personality and eventually began their life together. An exceptional delight has been the fact that their personal relationship has translated into a productive and successful professional partnership as well, that not only contributes to their intellectual growth, but also helps them realize their passion.

After gaining experience of working with a startup, Rohini quit her job and wanted to start something in the field of design – her true interest. Pramod, on the other hand, had been working in the field of marketing, travelling extensively. It was in this process that he realized the value of learning through real life experiences.

"It was as though an entire world opened up before me. I could clearly see the huge gap between our conventional methods of learning and the real life challenges we face," recalls Pramod, accounting for what led him to leave the conventional steady job and reach out for more.

Encouraged that they should do something in the space of alternate learning, when Pramod pitched the idea to Rohini, she was immediately hooked. Although there was the risk of financial problems if both quit their jobs, Rohini was extremely enterprising and broad-minded to encourage the idea. Hence, after a prolonged incubation with careful research and planning, the duo began their entrepreneurial journey in January 2013, organizing their first pilot module. Officially coming into shape as a company registered in March 2013, the passionate couple brought to life their brain child – Kitki.

At Kitki, passions were combined with an inherent need to transform the learning processes of the young generation.

"Our fascination for learning and our love for board games helped us come up with great fun games that are quite addictive, but at the same time based on educational concepts," Rohini speaks with excitement about the core of Kitki and the extraordinary games they have created with the principle of creating a learning experience. "Unlike other products currently in this space, these are not jigsaw puzzles, quizzes or activity kits. So one can play the games again and again and learn something new each time." So far, Kitki has created gaming experiences around the subject of chemistry, geometry and Indian history.

Endorsing real life experiences as a method to grow, they explain the attachment they feel with the cause that the enterprise is aimed at addressing. Deriving inspiration from the conventional methods of learning as an opportunity to learn something new in an effective and productive manner, they relate Kitki to a window of opportunity that is not available on conventional platforms.

"When a student does not connect with what is being taught in class, he keeps staring outside the window. We are that window of opportunity and choice that can educate and help you grow, with a new experience each time. Hence the name 'kitki' in Tamil, 'khidki' in Hindi," Rohini simplifies the fundamentals behind the name and idea of their business model, which is both entertaining and educative.

While one might easily be able to understand and appreciate the concept of Kitki as an alternate space of learning, it might still be unconventional to see life partners coming together as business partners. However, the duo has set a successful example within the fast-rising space of startups to establish how efficient and fruitful such a partnership can be. Rohini's experience helps them in planning the marketing efforts, while Pramod brings his experience as a management consultant to help in following some of the best practices in managing a business. While the two bring a diverse set of expertise to the table for Kitki, it is their exemplary compatibility that makes a perfect balance. Describing the business and its requirements, Pramod talks about the enterprise and their roles:

"There are four main departments – game ideas and play mechanics, artwork, manufacturing, and sales and marketing. While I take care of the ideation, Rohini is a champion when it comes to turning these ideas into reality. These two roles go hand-in-hand and we are really glad that our skills matched them perfectly."

When the duo reflect on people from other startups, especially from their own industry, the challenge of finding partners with compatibility and such deep understanding of each other's ideas is a clear indicator of how simple and convenient this experience has been for them. Having designed three successfully running games in a period of one-and-a-half years, the two have found confidence in not only their own strength, but also in each other in pursuit of their mission to reaching out to as many children as possible and becoming an integrated part of the learning process for the future generation.

But what appears to be a steady climb for the couple at work and home now, has seen its share of challenges that had them trudging together through tough times. The duo had initially set out to make Kitki a model of experiential learning, and tried to tie up with schools by conducting workshops.

"While organizing such workshops, we realized how effective game mechanics were in stimulating the young minds and how the whole class participated actively. We took the hint and started working on play-based learning," reflects Rohini on how things evolved from principle to practice. However, even when this decision had been reached, creating great games did not come easy. "With so much prototyping, play-testing, game mechanics and design iterations that went into developing these games, it took us a year-and-a-half to create our first three games – Three Sticks (on geometry), Escape EVIL (on chemistry) and Samrat (on Indian history)."

Even as the couple struggled to give shape to their dream, they had to face a few other challenges from their immediate environment. While their parents were shocked and uncomfortable about their plan of quitting their jobs and jumping into something so unusual, they did not protest and this came as a symbolic representation of the kind of resistance they would have to face with other stake holders, especially for raising funds.

"We did not have any external funding for a while. Using up all our savings was also not enough when it came to scaling up. This is when our friends and families came in together to show their confidence and support for us and helped us sail through the initial days," Pramod speaks with immense gratitude.

Even when ideation and production had attained a considerable stability, bringing schools on board to bring about this change in their orthodox methods of learning was not easy. With every passing struggle came immense learning and experience, making Rohini and Pramod root themselves stronger. Just like their motivation for Kitki, they also believed that once the parents started experiencing the value of the games, they themselves would become a medium of awareness and promotion of the brand and spread the credibility of this unique experiential learning. Despite the struggles, the duo has come out with valuable experiences that have helped them stabilize.

"When starting a business, it makes sense to hear and pay attention to everything that customers say. If we took the subtle hints that we got from the schools initially, we would have been able to pivot to the product model much earlier," speaks Pramod with a visible sense of maturity. It is with these elements of learning that the couple has been working to bring a wider growth and popularity in the brand and its reach.

As recognition came, so did an open attitude in the market as well as support from various platforms. Recalling their significant victory with an international platform for fund raising, Rohini talks about the experience of their crowdfunding campaign with Indiegogo, "Not only did we get immense financial support from the campaign, it was also a great confidence booster. The achievement helped us validate the concept of Kitki and put us out there on an international platform with many interested parents, schools and children, thus making it relatively easy for us to pitch for partnership with educational institutes."

Although catering to an exclusive segment of educative gaming, Kitki also positions its games like any other board game, making them accessible in both retail toy stores as well as online stores. While the two have been working extensively, handling all aspects of the enterprise by themselves, they do hire people from time to time as interns, whenever required. Defining the key to their stability as unconditional understanding, both Rohini and Pramod explain that the motivation behind this perusal is their utter passion in what they're doing that differentiates their enterprise from the ordinary definitions of work. Both do what they enjoy doing. Although being partners both in personal life as well as professional, differences are bound to happen.

"Conflicts do come back home with us sometimes, as there are no boundaries between work and home. But we definitely are working towards a balance. We have come to realize that conflicts lead to a discussion that is for the betterment of Kitki, hence encouraged," confesses Rohini with a candid smile

With diversity brought to the table, the pair handles different aspects. While Pramod's day is spent with meetings and travel, Rohini spends the day with online promotion, social media and brand building, etc. This, like many other examples in their life, clearly goes on to show how differences have aligned in favour of their dream of making Kitki the top brand for educational games in the country. While accepting that more funds could have helped tremendously in realizing this dream with more efficiency and effectiveness, Rohini explains that they have to a lot of investments to promote the business without the luxury of extravagant funding. But the couple is confident that all challenges will only help them build a stronger enterprise and things will iron out eventually.

Looking at future growth as the only target, irrespective of the hurdles, Rohini and Pramod are extremely excited about how well the games have turned out. Taking things together with categorical steps, they are currently focusing on streamlining the sales and marketing channels, before turning to making more such games on a wide range of concepts from academic subjects to career choices to global issues. "A few years down the lane, we plan to start game-based and experiential learning centers where kids (and even adults) can have fun, experiment, learn through activities and may be even solve real world challenges," Pramod reveals excitedly.

While acknowledging other players in the market who are working on the same lines of gaming platforms, the industry holds a very wide scope and in fact the opportunity of catching up and sharing experiences is something which brings a healthy and holistic attitude instead of a competitive, cut-throat one. With appreciation for every little achievement as a steady mark of success and motivation, the couple believes in celebrating their partnership – the moments of glory as well as challenges. "Every little milestone achieved together has been a moment of pride," adds Pramod.

Describing their struggle and experiences together – from collecting the first funding from well-wishers, to the first manufactured game, first media coverage to the first deal, the duo oozes confidence and passion for the cause and believe that every step has been a sign of way forward, making sure they're on the right track. Setting as an example for aspiring entrepreneurs to follow, the couple has shown new definitions of partnership that they have accomplished. With each other's faith and understanding, it is nothing short of a feat that inspires many others to break the rules and create their own paths.

---

kitki

To know more about interesting games and innovative ways of easy learning, visit www.kitki.in or Facebook: /openkitki.

"Fall in love with the person who enjoys your madness and partakes in it. Your passion can take you to heights you had never imagined."

*When **Rajat & Madhumita** gave up their lucrative jobs to teach, little did they know it would lead to a major change – experimental games that make learning a fun process. **MadRat** has to its credit more than hundred board games that have reached close to a million families.*

All Work is All Play! – MADRAT GAMES

By Rajat & Madhumita

When people begin to wonder what their purpose in life is, or where they are headed in the larger picture of the universe, it is called an existential awakening. Some of them get stuck in the endless webs of inquisition, while some go on an inward-bound journey of soul searching. However, there are a few, who, mindful of the enigma of the universe, actively seek to explore its depths, while still probing through the questions and aiming to address them, if not answer them in entirety. It is these people who have put themselves out there in the world to take conscious actions to add value to life. Even though this endeavour may be intended at bringing them peace personally, they often end up contributing to the betterment of the society. With absolute fascination, exemplary dedication, and a knack to break away from conventions, a couple set out on their own journey of discovering themselves. What followed next not only surprised everyone, but turned upside down the definition of what it is to be successful and happy in one's life.

A shy student, pursuing his degree in engineering from one of the most prestigious colleges of the country, was all set to make his mark in the world. A dynamic, outgoing girl in his class chanced to be his partner is several projects and laboratory sessions. The duo was teased by friends, and the two were conscious when together, and yet always ended up having an entertaining conversation with each other. And before their graduation ended, this unlikely pair had already become close. Their beautiful combination of synergies flowered into a beautiful relationship that resulted in many more wonderful things to follow

Rajat and Madhumita, two engineers with extraordinary skills and determinant passion, have been evolving through their journey beyond academics, profession or even personal goals. Rajat went out of India to pursue a Master's degree with the aim of gaining more knowledge and exposure in his field of interest. This was where a new and inspiring journey of his life began. Turning towards more spiritual and existential questions, he was driven towards a holistic and conscious school of thought. Madhumita, on the other hand, continued her work back in India. However, the couple would spend long hours discussing their experiences and learnings. The distance did them no good, and thus, with Rajat stumbling through the completion of his degree and Madhumita anxiously awaiting his return, the duo finally got married. Like a story from the movies, the boy and girl had to go through turmoil to convince their parents. Hailing from different social backgrounds, the opposition was bound to happen; but their commitment won in the end. However, it appeared as though challenges were destined to be their closest followers for a long time. With Rajat still in the middle of his Master's and Madhumita's US visa having been rejected, it would have appeared that the two would be disheartened and would hold it against their destinies. However, as unpredictable as the couple has been, their responses and attitude through trying times has also been extremely optimistic and praiseworthy.

"Whatever unfolded before us was a part of the larger scheme. In fact, I am glad that things turned out the way they did. Otherwise, we probably may have been stuck in the rituals of a mundane and unsatisfying lifestyle," Rajat speaks in retrospection.

Despite being excellent at what they did in their respective subjects or at work, both Rajat and Madhumita shared this sentiment of a certain dissatisfaction clouding their lives. They had the luxury of studying in some of the best places in the world, were headed towards a future together that would be both financially and socially stable and secure, and seemed to tick right on all the check boxes in the definition of successful people in the purview of most conventional people.

"It was almost like a vacant space lurked in both our minds. It didn't feel like we were on the right path, adding values to ourselves and the larger cosmos of being. Something did not feel right and it had to change," Madhumita reflects on the beginning of the transition that prompted the couple to make drastic decisions in their lives. In the process of exploring his existential quest, Rajat had taken to reading different philosophers. Out of these, J. Krishnamurti held his thoughts deeply and seemed to attract him as an inherent calling. It was then that the couple decided to quit their conventional hang-ups, entirely give up on their preferences for a comfort zone, and move to the Rishi Valley School to teach children.

"My friends and family thought we had lost it; such qualified engineers giving up on the most lucrative opportunities in the world to become teachers! But we knew what we wanted, and took the leap of faith!" he exclaims with a generous smile.

During their experience of teaching children for a period of about four years, the couple realized the gaps, challenges and opportunities that came along in the process. One of the most prominent lessons were about the modes of learning.

"It was so surprising to see that the children who would be finicky, cranky or distracted within minutes into a class while a lesson was being taught, suddenly transformed into these dynamites of skill, concentration and determination when they got around to different forms of games!" Madhumita speaks from observation.

With this learning as the base of their idea, the duo started experimenting with different methods of imparting lessons to children. They would involve more games and activities related to the subject and conduct classes in very non-conventional ways. Even during their session breaks or vacations, Rajat and Madhumita would be busy designing or innovating some or the other form of experimental modules for their lessons involving gaming tools. The results were astounding! Not only was the class performing much better in general, but the learning experience also opened up the blocks of many children and helped their overall development.

It was thus that the foundation of a much larger initiative was laid. Having shifted to an entirely activity and games-oriented module, without books, their science lab had turned into a work station for some of the most unique and clever innovations that the duo had been designing and successfully applying in their lessons. With the innovation of their board games, Rajat and Madhumita also realized the potential of such a platform they had created and its larger implications. They began to understand the fact that they could take their idea of learning through games across different schools a notch higher, not only in India, but also on a global level. Besides, they also felt that having got this opportunity and privilege; they owed it to bring forward such an idea of learning in the world, where a lot of stress is being laid on competitive, cut-throat and materialistic learning. And thus, with a mission to take this learning and gaming platform worldwide, began a new journey of teaching, learning, innovating and enterprising. Rajat and Madhumita formed their own enterprise and launched it by the name MadRats.

"Our vision became to make childhood calmer, wiser, happier… using the power of play!" enunciates Rajat. With an implication of reforming the mode of education so that it becomes more enticing and value adding for children, MadRats was all about fun, excitement and learning. Swanky and enticing, the name actually holds a lot of history for the couple. Back in their college days, even before their courtship period, the duo was teased by the term 'Madrats' – an acronym for both their names. The term stuck on and continued to be a part of their lives. Coincidently, resonating the sentiment of a little bit of unconventional excitement, Madrats suited perfectly well for the unique gaming model of a learning project. With a catchy pronunciation, it appealed to the kids, and eventually, the name grew on to become a trademark of all the innovative games that the couple created.

What began as the launch of a limited range of games as a pilot, turned into an extensive and diverse collection of board games.

"At MadRat we created close to a hundred new board games and have reached close to a million families," Madhumita gleams with pride. With the duo having gotten together with the best of their skills, their combination turned into a productive and lucrative affair.

"Madhumita is a natural teacher. She has the acumen to connect with children at a level that they are comfortable with. I, on the other hand, have a keen interest in research. After a phase of researching and experimentation that had given them a deep understanding of the subject they had been exploring, the duo managed to present themselves on a prestigious platform that not only gave them a good opportunity to test their standard amidst the best entrepreneurs, but also got a considerable visibility and push to promote their model and brand. Having moved efficiently with their marketing flow, MadRat went to retail and expanded from twenty stores and three products to two thousand stores and a hundred products in less than two years. Today MadRat has reached more than a million children, been awarded as one of the Top Ten Indian Innovators by the Government of India, Top Ten Startups in Asia, featured prominently by all major publications, and is well-respected in the Indian startup ecosystem.

However, what may appear to be smoothened grounds of a successful enterprise today has emerged from a rigorous journey with many challenges. While breaking the convention and comfort of lucrative, stable careers was not easy, to be able to make something substantial of their alternative choice was a responsibility they had taken upon themselves.

"Selling board games in the era of digital revolution was a fairly long shot. Not only is the popularity of such games going down drastically, but to be able to break the clutter of this segment to stand out was also extremely challenging," Rajat explains.

As if it wasn't enough, MadRat faced another challenge. With a game that held its base in the Hindi language, the acceptability was highly unpredictable.

"When everybody in India wants everything from their magazines to their number plates in English, we were pitching for a Hindi board game, and it sounded ridiculous to most people. But we had to stick strong to our vision," Rajat speaks determinately. Even on a personal front, the lack of confidence from people around, and the struggle between the tough choices that the husband and wife had to make between their personal thoughts and their actions together, was plenty of reason for confusion and dilemma. However, as Madhumita fondly admits, the couple found strength in each other and promised to sail through, no matter what.

Despite the polar disparity in the two personality types, Rajat and Madhumita have complemented like Yin and Yan. A combination of impulse and planning, research and creativity, they have been fitting in each other's life like a perfect jigsaw puzzle.

"He lifts my spirits when I am down, and I pull him forward if he is keeping low. We bring the best of both our individual traits into this equation – both professional and personal," Madhumita speaks fondly. Although revealing that there really is no boundary between the personal and professional in their lives, the couple counts themselves lucky to be pursuing what their heartfelt passion is. Not regarding MadRats as some place where they 'work', they believe that it is as personal to them as each other, and hence there never really has been a defined work or home front for either of them. Sharing an equation of matured respect for each other, the duo reflect a symbiotic relationship where they are uniquely dependent and yet independent. With mutual appreciation, while Madhumita dotes upon Rajat as the wise man who has a keen sense of observation and eye for details, Rajat affectionately calls her a superwoman who juggles between all responsibilities at work, at home, maintaining relations with her friends and family, and now nurturing to add a new member to their family. In awe of her exemplary attitude towards perfection, he feels proud to draw inspiration from her. Clearly, this equation not only helps nourish a healthy relationship between the dynamic duo, but also spills into an environment they have organically cultivated in MadRats. With about fifty-two employees as a part of the family, the venture functions like a symbiotic organism working towards a common vision. Not only are the employees a dedicated set of people, but they also create a culturally and behaviorally conscious environment that feels responsible for the cause they are working towards.

"There are two kinds of entrepreneurs – ones where if they grow, only they grow themselves, and others where if they grow, the whole ecosystem grows with them. MadRat as a company and us as individuals, have always strived to be the latter, aware that we are part of a community," speaks Rajat with an awe inspiring air of consciousness. Their next project breaks the norms, even by the standards of Madrats, and it has the potential of revolutionary standards. Catering to the evolving patterns of human behaviour as well as technological advancement, their latest experiment aims to combine the best of both worlds – technology with physical games.

"It is interesting to see the culmination of the diverse background that include computer science, teaching and creating physical games with the new age wearable computing coming together," exclaims Madhumita with regards to their idea of gaming that they have been working on for the last two years. Wearable game now known as supersuit.io recently made it debut at CES in Vegas. The duo were recently blessed with baby boy "Joy" who sneaked to the event and became the youngest participant.

Dedication, passion, surrender, evolution, and an appreciable degree of humility reflect in this out of the ordinary couple. With their skills and education, they have risen to a rare standard of service and vision – a combination hard to find in the materialistic world of today. They complement each other, support each other, protect each other and guide each other too. As a couple who believes in life as a constant process of learning, they sure are headed in the right direction to create a platform of learning which is holistic, futuristic, and yet at the same time ingrained with the value system that seems to be fast disappearing from the world. Not only do they make a couple to draw inspiration from in their expertise of entrepreneurship, but also set up a high benchmark as responsible entrepreneurs, who are working on something far beyond their personal goals.

Explore MadRat games at www.madratgames.com and Facebook: /madratgames to gift your loved ones some of the most fun ways of learning.

Madhurita & Yuvraj *are both veterinarians who wished to work for the betterment of animals. They found* **MYvets** *and have since then designed animal shelters, plans for zoos, set up animal care models for reptile parks, and a fully automated wildlife rescue ambulance, among other achievements.*

The Wild Life – MYVETS

By Madhurita & Yuvraj

One of the very conventional and predictable ways of living would be to find someone who you can connect with, have common interests and build a life partnership with them. This is conventionally what most Indians do. What would be a natural course of action to follow is to pursue your respective careers with considerable amounts of sacrifices here and there and find a middle path that can work for the personal and professional lives of both the partners. By regular standards, this would mean that the average aspirations and requirements of a happy married life are being met in their lives. Once these traditional needs of a couple are met, most people find satiation in both the work and home front. Such is the life of an average Indian couple. While nothing can be pointed out as particularly wrong or right in such lives, it is not hard to miss that in the bigger picture, there is a missing consequence. As individuals, as well as a couple, there are endeavours and accomplishments that can go on to define who you are and what you choose to become. To discover this side of you needs a certain degree of strength, risk taking and support that can help you sustain in the long run. There are, however, a few exceptions to this trend when things are taken in control by a few right people at the right moments of their lives. The life of one such couple that changed not just the course of their lives but also resulted in altering the course of an entire industry of the country is a story worth sharing.

A very seemingly regular couple, Madhurita and Yuvraj, met through what would appear to be a typical Indian match making process. Dr Yuvraj R. Kaginkar was a renowned expert in veterinarian science, working as the CEO of Sarama Petcare, paid handsomely and respected universally for his work and research. Dr Madhurita was happily established with her profession in London when she was proposed as the match of the accomplished doctor. What attracted her to India right on the day of her wedding is still what most people would find hard to do, but destiny brought Madhurita and Yuvraj to come together and get married to settle down in the bustling city of Mumbai.

"I think my first feeling for Yuvraj was that of fascination. I was in awe with this person who had accomplished so much, who shared the same passion and affection for animals as I did. It just felt right to know that I could spend my life with someone like him," recalls Madhurita with a smile on her face.

With time, the duo discovered that it wasn't just their professional interest that had them attracted to each other; in fact, the principles about their own perspectives in life, and with their dreams about the future, the couple found many deeply embedded fundamentals that had common roots for the two of them.

Madhurita is the sort of person who can be defined as dynamic, extrovert and someone who is enterprising in building contacts, convincing people and building relations. Yuvraj is a man of details who understands the depth of the technical nuances of his work, with his experience and knowledge. Together, they make an excellent pair of work and voice. Under the given circumstances, where Madhurita was seeking out to start something of her own, finding a partner as supportive and collaborative as Yuvraj turned into a circumstantial catalyst. With an aim to start an independent work for the larger umbrella of animal care through organized and optimized consultancy, she pitched her idea and model to Yuvraj, which was both accepted and appreciated by her counterpart. In fact, coming out in complete support, he stepped up to help her out in the endeavour. This idea was deliberated upon for a period of almost a year where everything from homework to paper work was set down in ink. And with an amalgamation of their perfect bond and understanding emerged what has become today a one of its kind enterprise in the country, MYvets. Under this umbrella, the couple has formed MYvet Integrated Solutions Pvt Ltd, MYvets4Pets Animal Hospital, as well as MYvets Charitable Trust and Research Centre. Breaking conventions and redefining the platform of animal care, the learned stalwarts of the veterinary industry have come far with milestones of achievements, whether it has been about introducing ground breaking technologies for animal care in hospitals, or designing zoos of international standards.

A perfect combination of both their skills and experience, the name MYvets in itself reflects their joint effort in the endeavour. Taking the initial letters of their names, Madhurita and Yuvraj have formulated a brand with a name that radiates the true spirit of their brain child, taking ownership of a large gap in animal care, and instilling it with their passion and dedication.

"There were a lot of issues that needed to be address in this sector. People have been working of course, but we could sense a desperate calling for an organized and quality solution for animal care at a macro level." Yuvraj talks about the importance of building a platform like MYvets in a space where conventional assistance for animal care was available either through established institutes or small independent consultants. In forming MYvets, not only did this unconventional couple put a concrete step forward towards their personal passion, but also paved the way into reshaping professional animal care in the mainstream arena. With the motivation to give back to the world than draw from it, the couple has dedicated its skills and resources into elevating the standards of animal care by national as well as international standards.

Whether it has been about acquiring their major projects for designing animal shelters, master planning for zoos or setting up animal care models for reptile parks, or their remarkable work in creating the first fully automated wildlife rescue ambulance, Madhurita and Yuvraj have achieved milestones, one after another. It has won them national as well as international acclamation, and brought them to a position of repute as a brand. However, this healthy picture of an independent and path breaking enterprise has not been an easy ride. The two have had to struggle through their share of challenges and anxieties to make it this far in the run.

"The initial idea of leaving behind the conventional path to form a startup in this sector was full of apprehension. The risk was high and there was practically no existing method to learn and practice from – this was a big challenge for us," recalls Madhurita about the initial days of homework. The financial requirement for the enterprise was massive and turned into a major challenge for the couple. To be able to keep the salaries and rent going, they gave many things up.

"When we were filing for our very first tender, they wanted a financial guarantee. It was very difficult for us to accumulate such a large amount, but we did not want to give up at that stage, knowing we had both the skills and the experience to win this tender. We did win the tender eventually, but at the cost of a huge financial stake," speaks a candid Madhurita.

Putting everything at stake, the couple went on to pursue their passion with utmost determination, even at the cost of professional jealousy and discouragement from established colleagues.

"There was a lot of opposition from people of the sector. They tried to tell us that the idea wouldn't work, that it would lead to a lot of problems amongst our contemporaries. In fact, there was a lot of jealousy when we landed our first tender. It even brought us to a point where we were thinking of quitting," she recalls the past. As if things were not on the edge already, there were expectations from family that had to be faced.

"My dad, being a scientist himself, wanted me to get into academics or research. It was quite difficult for him to accept that his daughter was going to be an entrepreneur," she shares, recollecting the dilemma. Although the duo admits that there were a few substantial moves in marketing and human resource building that they skipped due to lack of entrepreneurial experience and the luxury of finance, however, with faith and confidence, the challenges were slowly overcome with support from friends and family and eventually MYvets started rising exponentially on its path of success.

The first mark of success came with the contract for the largest zoo consultancy of the country for a land of five hundred acres in Jammu & Kashmir. Since then, there has been no looking back. In the times when recognition and acclamation was trickling in slowly despite their services of best quality, some breakthrough events changed the game for the couple and MYvets.

"We had pitched the wildlife rescue ambulance to many private, public and corporate stalwarts, but nobody was able to understand the importance and need of this pragmatic approach to Wildlife-Human Conflict Resolution. It was frustrating at that point to see that people were not open to receiving new technology. However, it was at this time that the esteemed Tata Trust, and

Mr. Ratan Tata himself took interest in our product and ensured that we got optimum promotion and support to bring the model to use," recalls Yuvraj with both delight and relief.

With the association and promotion of an organization of such philanthropic and respectable stature, the credibility of MYvets was validated numinously. With a sense of accomplishment instilled with the brand, Madhurita and Yuvraj went on to add several feathers to their hats. Along with being associated with the State Forest Department of Maharashtra and having done many unique wildlife projects with Sanjay Gandhi National Park, MYvets has also been accredited for designing of enrichment plan and devices for a Leopard Rescue Centre (published by the Zoological Association of America) and architectural designing for extension of the lion safari and tiger safari. Within a short span of time, Yuvraj has also added significant inputs with responsibility of master planning of the zoo and leopard safari in two hundred acres and conceptual planning, architectural designing and master plan of the largest reptile house at Kolhapur.

The couple went ahead with the world's first species conservation project under Habitat Restoration for Raj Bhavan, with the initiative of Hon'ble Governor of Maharahstra Shri C. Vidyasagar Rao, with financial support from Tata Trusts for wild Peacocks, as their numbers were dwindling due to habitat shrinkage and predators. The Peacock Conservation Project was conceptualized and designed by Dr. Madhurita and Dr. Yuvraj, and stands as a main attraction now at Raj Bhavan. The couple have made the ecological conditions congenial for better survival and breeding of the peacocks; the results have been outstanding, with increase in the number of peacocks in Mumbai now.

Dr. Madhurita and Dr. Yuvraj always believed in novel technologies, and in the year 2016, they innovated World's first "Wildlife Rescue Bike" for Leopard – Human Conflicts Mitigation;

Tiger – Human Conflicts Mitigation for Thane forest; Tadoba Tiger Reserve in Maharshtra for safe patrolling and tranquilization of wildlife during conflicts. This is now a breakthrough technology under their Make in India campaign, and has got the eye of both National/International Media, and scientific journals.

The couple today have 3 patents in wildlife technology and many unique projects to their credit in wildlife conservation and wildlife technology in India. Dr. Madhurita was chosen as a top-working woman in reptile conservation for BBC, which itself is strong validation of their work in their sector of work.

Accentuating their years of experience and in-depth knowledge, Madhurita and Yuvraj have built a unique selling point for MYvets that none other in this sector has yet been able to offer. Presenting business models and designs for zoos and aviaries that is self-sustained, with added conservation value including special features like creating awareness in society about wildlife, the venture offers modern designs with enrichment of enclosures along with the services of MYvets4pets Animal Hospital.

"We follow international protocols and incorporate best management practices and hospitalization facilities for pets, wild animals and birds. This is something no one else has been able to claim in this country," declares a proud Yuvraj with sheer confidence in his venture.

A deeper probe into their work life reveals more than just skills and experience as the key to their success. The exemplary partnership of the two has been beyond doubt the core of this accomplishment. With unconditional support and understanding of each other's strengths and thinking, they form a team that is not only compatible, but also complementary. "Madhurita is excellent with business acquisition and management skills. She handles meeting with people, communicating with clients and completing the feedback cycle. I, on the other hand, concentrate on the technical domain of the services. So it's like we have the best of both worlds at home!" Yuvraj laughs heartily.

His statement reveals more than a zestful emotion in echoing the true mantra of success while working with family. Despite working on different verticals of the venture, the couple still involve each other in all major decisions and discussions, while respecting each other's opinions and choices. With a stable balance between individual authority and partnering compatibility, Madhurita and Yuvraj have raised the enterprise from a struggling startup into an internationally acclaimed organization with over twenty-two core team members, and celebrated consultants from across the country.

The two have managed to build a spine for their entrepreneurial dream by keeping their personal interests intact. Just as much as their professional accomplishment has reached a zenith, the dynamic duo has also achieved a bond based on deep affection and respect for each other. Despite the struggle of their entrepreneurial journey, the hurdles have only helped them learn more about each other and strive through each day despite the differences. Just as their professional domain is an amalgamation of both individual and team work complementing each other, so is their personal equation. Juggling between household chores, needs of the family and taking care of an excessively demanding occupation, the duo also try to find personal balance.

"Responsibilities and differences can get overwhelming sometimes, especially for me as a mother, because giving utmost care to my young one is just as much of a priority as is MYvets; they are both our babies but it is a struggle that keeps us on our toes," Madhurita exhales with an experience that reveals her everyday fight to excel. "But with open communication and support from Yuvraj, things become much easier and positive for the both of us."

Battling the predictable challenges of an entrepreneurial lifestyle of unending work, the two share responsibilities at home and manage to take time out for each other, as well as their personal hobbies.

MYvets has evolved from their brain child into a flourishing enterprise, and has given the couple a sense of authority to advise aspiring entrepreneur couples who still struggle with the apprehensions of working with their life partners.

Yuvraj speaks with insight, "The idea is to understand the market you are about to get into and do your homework well. Once you think you are ready, dive in without a doubt in your head. There will be a lot of challenges, but don't let fear overcome you." Speaking from first-hand experience, Madhurita talks about cherishing the bond with the life partner as a business partner, as it comes with blind trust, mutual understanding and respect. Referring to the testing times as a litmus test for a lasting relationship, she reinstates the reason why she has managed to bring her bright idea to the level of success with the standing support of her husband. MYvets is not only an example of path-breaking service in an industry that could not have imagined finding such a creative entrepreneurial platform, but it more importantly reflects the spirit of the couple that stands behind it, with their symbiotic relation and consistently growing passion for work and life.

To know more about the duo and their exemplary work over the years, do visit www.myvetsol.com.

Addressing the challenge of making healthy living a part of one's lifestyle, **Mitalee & Saurabh** *started off* **Oomph Nutrition** *and work as an online portal to provide healthcare solutions.*

A Matter of Well-being – OOMPH NUTRITION

By Mitalee & Saurabh

In this new age, with startups being a trend, most aspiring entrepreneurs seem to go with the flow and tend to implement a model which is the safest and most lucrative for them. Often services of the enterprise, its quality and authenticity is compromised or largely ignored. As long as the venture skirts around a fad, it is most likely that the target audience will more or less accept it. While this may appeal to people as a commercial aspect, there are some who beg to differ on the grounds of fundamental integrity, both for their business, as well as their sector. In such circumstances, people can either continue in their profession, be vocal about the vastly popular farce being propagated by their peers, or step in with active intervention to modify this trend and bring actual meaning to their experience and knowledge through transforming the misgivings gaining popularity in their line of profession. When such individuals step in to take charge, you can clearly see a distinct phenomenon building. Through fate, destiny or sheer passion to make a difference, one such phenomenon has come in the form of a partnership between an accomplished couple that has resolved to change the way health, fitness and medical well-being is being marketed by business models across the country.

Mitalee, a post-graduate in dietetics and nutrition was an established professional in her stable career. Saurabh, on the other hand, holds a Master's degree in Business Administration and has been working with organizations across dimensions with his skills and experience.

"We met for the first time in the most traditional manner: two people introduced for an arranged marriage. Our families had connected and asked us to meet each other in a restaurant and figure out whether we'd be compatible. And we did!" Mitalee unveils how it all began.

It was then in the very meeting, as she recalls, that the two clicked and the foundations of an ever-lasting partnership was laid. Following their instincts, the two found faith in each other and got married in 2012. That's when the real story began.

As the duo got closer, understanding each other, their aspirations in life, skills and strengths, they realized that though they both categorically belonged to different sectors of professions, their fundamental principles and ambitions were extremely aligned with each other. They both aimed to make a difference and do something impactful in the lives of people, while working on their own terms, without slaving out to corporate giants.

"As I got to know Mitalee better, I realized she is extremely passionate about what she does. It was evident that she was very unhappy with the way things are being commercialized in her sector of diet, healthcare and well-being. Her discontentment with the farce and fake services in the name of these mushroomed health clinics was very valid. I often encouraged her to dig for solutions," Saurabh retrospects about the seeding thoughts of the venture. A passion for setting things right and the well-placed support and encouragement brought Mitalee to take the bold and difficult decision of leaving her job and venturing out to build her own startup – a place where genuine, credible and relevant services could be provided to needful clients, to help them build a healthy and positive lifestyle, something that is a rising crisis in today's scenario. And hence, with Mitalee's initiative and Saurabh's immense support was born their joint venture – Oomph Nutrition.

Addressing the challenge of the mass sprouting of health clinics across the country has become both the ambition as well as the unique selling point of Oomph Nutrition. A holistic service that provides for health-based fitness management, weight management or medical fitness management programs based on the needs of respective clients, Oomph Nutrition is dedicated to offering specific, customized and relevant remedies of health and well-being, rather than simply selling factory made health packs to customers.

"The root of health is in one's lifestyle. One has to understand a client's habits, strengths, lifestyle, habits, what they can do or cannot do, things they can do conveniently or enjoy doing, etc. When you make an effort to understand the person, your solution can be designed around that and hence can be implemented most effectively," Mitalee explains the uniqueness and efficiency of Oomph with such a simple mantra that it compels one to rethink a lot about the so-called fitness regime one follows blindly.

As if the services themselves were not enough to make the enterprise a popular one, a cleverly thought brand value also adds to its credit. Evoking an aspiration of the 'X' factor, the name calls out for exactly what the target audience is looking for. An external and internal confidence that comes with being healthy and happy is something that the founder understands and appreciates in her sector of work. Thus, bringing people to a stage where they can appreciate their health, appearance and find a new confidence to embrace life, the venture is dedicated to catering to its clients on a personal level. This makes Oomph Nutrition not just about health packages, but a more inclusive way of life for one's well-being.

The beginning of this game-changing phenomenon came with a deep insight of the current problems, or a well-based structure of knowledge and experience. It was further complemented with a well-thought process flow, planning and homework by the couple. Besides analyzing the current market, target audience and competitors, a great deal of effort has also been put in for financial planning, marketing and advertising strategies and risk assessment by the duo. Even while setting the basic model of the enterprise, the couple worked on all verticals together. It was a contemplated decision that Mitalee should dive nose deep into program building and initiating the startup while Saurabh continued working full time in his job to ensure cushioning for financial shocks. This way, they believe, not only was Mitalee more free to take decisions without the burden of financial pressure, but a strong plan B was in place in case things needed a different course of action.

"While the intention behind Saurabh's decision to continue working for a while was so that we are financially not troubled, a wonderful outcome of this decision was that many things eased out themselves just knowing that he had my back," Mitalee speaks with a sense of contentment.

It is only after the enterprise had gained a certain level of sustainability and the couple managed to build enough capital to keep the business rolling without external support, that Saurabh decided to quit his job and join the venture full time and support Mitalee in marketing and advertising.

While growth has been consistent and appreciable in the lives of Mitalee and Saurabh, it is hard to ignore the hurdles that they have crossed in order to come this far. With a well thought out decision to refrain from external funding, the liberty to invest was limited in the initial days and choices had to be made stringently. For marketing and PR building, conventional methods turned out to be an uncertain and costly affair. Also, Mitalee felt that setting up a permanent set-up with employees to support on regular basis was not turning out to be a lucrative model for Oomph. With these issues lying ahead of them, the risks needed to be reduced considerably and efficiency of the business had to be ensured without compromising with the quality. This is when a solution emerged in the form of initiating Oomph Nutrition in the form of an online portal.

"We were initially apprehensive about whether our clients would be open to taking consultancy online, for a matter which is so personal. But the response came as an extremely pleasant surprise. Not only were we being sought after by people across geographies, but our accessibility from anywhere, at any time, was something people began to enjoy incredibly," explains Saurabh.

Breaking the stereotype of physically limiting clinics stationed in the metro cities, Oomph Nutrition has risen to reach out to clients even in the smaller towns and makes it effortlessly simple for clients to access from anywhere, without having to go out of the way or disrupt their regular schedules. Addressing the problem of expenditure in capital, rentals, etc., that the startup could have found difficulty in affording, the online forum has benefited them by helping cut costs. Overcoming the challenges and risks involved, Mitalee and Saurabh have worked together, understanding the strengths that they have drawn from each other as well as their circumstances. While acknowledging the support that the two have found from their families, they talk about the encouragement they have found from them,

"In most cases, families are not very happy when you want to quit your job and start something of your own. But our families have encouraged us to explore our calling, but also showed complete faith in us. They have supported us in every way possible, and this is something that has kept us going despite the challenges," Mitalee speaks with gratitude.

It is not surprising then that despite the many challenges and apprehensions, the dynamic duo has been able to break out of difficulties to achieve recognition and appreciation from their clients. Having been recognized for their entrepreneurial excellence by *The Economic Times,* the two have stuck to their principle of integrity and quality in service. Instead of exhausting resources in loud advertisement and brand value, they have focused on creating an experience that compels their clients to keep coming back for more.

"Our satisfied clients are our biggest brand ambassadors. Instead of hungrily running after more business, we just focus on keeping our clients happy, which in turn works for generating more business for us!" Saurabh speaks from experience. Having seen the business through its trying years, he now believes that a strong foundation is built by keeping an open attitude for growth. Not focusing on competition from several health clinics in the sector, Mitalee speaks with confidence with her ambition about being in a different zone, away from commercial race.

"We believe in an organic growth, we don't deal with aggressive competition or beating someone in the race. Our services are to add value to people's lives, that's what matters." It is not surprising therefore, when her attitude towards criticism is equally progressive as it helps her improve the quality of her work, hence being a real mark of achievement every time she manages to convert a problem into a strength.

Despite belonging to completely different sectors of education and experience, the two have proved their compatibility by showing faith in each other, understanding their strengths and skills, and utilizing them to the best of the needs in the enterprise. Their partnership feels complete with cooperation and understanding of each other's core, making the decision of working together to turn out to be the best combination ever. While Mitalee focuses on client product, dealing with the service end of the model, Saurabh, with his management education and experience, handles the business end, adding marketing strength with his acumen for technological aids in the enterprise. The two have learnt over the years to support each other through their independent and individual decisions and seem to have mastered the art of perfect balance by respecting each other's opinions and advice wherever appropriate.

"Most people we meet wonder how we manage to work with each other, the most common notion being that you can't work with family without spoiling relations. But I think if you can work with your family, there's no better solution. It just makes our life so much easier!" Mitalee continues candidly, "If I were working with an outsider, there would always be trust issues or concern of vested interests. Also, I am not sure Saurabh and I would have been able to understand each other's situation so deeply. But look at us now!"

Explaining their work equation as a strictly professional relation, the couple explains how the key to a perfect balance is not to melt the balance between work and home. While being absolutely passionate about their brain child, they make it a point to keep their personal life equally high on the priority list. Taking out time for their personal responsibilities and sharing chores and making decisions together are some basic things that the couple has come to appreciate.

Speaking with first-hand experience, Saurabh appreciates the opportunity of being able to partner up with his spouse in life and work. Dismissing the fear of working with one's life partner as a myth, he advises aspiring entrepreneurs to invest liberally into homework and research, as well as planning to increase cushions against risks in the initial phase as it helps to make big decisions with relative ease. True to their core of integrity and respect for life, the duo radiates a strong sense of acknowledgement and appreciation for each other, revealing a much deeper reason for the success of their endeavour. Not only has their bold decision of stepping up as entrepreneurs helped them pursue their passion, but has also helped them strengthen as a couple as well as individuals, making themselves a true example of overall well-being.

"When your relationship adds passion to your business
partnership, you can build an empire."

As the name in itself suggests, **Shortcircuit.in** is a one stop solution for quirky gifts and merchandise that is sure to steal hearts. **Vipul & Richa** bring a zing into the lives of consumers through their startup, which is funny and a pleasant break from the normalcy of life.

A Sure and Short Circuit! – SHORTCIRCUIT.IN

By Richa & Vipul

Predictable, stable, routine and regular – these are words most people aspire towards and probably achieve in their life's endeavours. Cluttered in purpose, expectations and relations with exactly the same definitions and parametres, there's no way of telling them apart in a crowd. Inconsequently then, such lives do not create any major event, nor cause any major change in the environment around them. But amidst such a crowd, rarely seen are some people who stand apart. In their purpose, methods, actions and even at the level of thoughts, they form a different eco-system altogether. Sometimes they emerge amidst us as individuals with resonance of their thoughts, other times as opportunities that brush our lives with their own essence. In either case, they are easy to spot, hard to ignore and impossible to forget. The life of one such unconventional duo has come into the public eye in the past few years and in their own unique, intriguing and inspiring way, they have touched many connections in people's lives in big and small ways, sending out little signals of joy, fun and creativity.

Vipul and Richa form the famous couple who have partnered up in life as well as in work. What brought them together was a sheer brush of luck, but what has brought them along so far has more to with complementing each other in life and in the business they have started as partners. You might think that it would take them a major life event to leave the stability of their lives to jump into a business. But free-spirited Richa will have you in no doubts about the free will and spontaneity that marks and guides her life.

"I was looking for an excuse to get away from angry bosses and a routined life. The idea of a startup came as a need to get away from boredom, and that is exactly what it is also focused on doing," she explains in a light spirit. So what came about as this creative couple's brain child? A whacky brand that offers the craziest, quirkiest and funniest products that bring humour and fun in people's lives. An enterprise that has been functioning for the last three years now, the venture reflects the ethos in its name – Short Circuit.

"If you see relationships as circuits, then you've got to see that they get criss-crossed, complicated and messed up with all the seriousness. So simply, to keep things simple, happy and short, we bring you Short Circuit," she adds her fun flavour.

As someone who looks for fun and creativity in every aspect of life, Richa talks about the monotony of most gift products in the market.

"They may have an aesthetic quotient through their designs and pattern, but I believe in the zing that comes with something funny, something hazardous in lieu of the normalcy of things."

Short Circuit is a dedicated range of gift items for those who have a taste for humour. With their primary clientele as corporates who believe in making the extra effort when it comes to choosing gifts for employees and clients, Short Circuit's products are created with an aim to make you smile and bring the relationship between the giver and receiver at ease. Personalized hand painted caricatures in nameplates, clocks, t-shirts, canvases, etc., are some of the unique products which can be given as gifts across any age limit and background that the engaging enterprise has to offer. Not a huge fan of strategic consumerism, the founders of the iconic brand believe their target audience to be anyone who belongs to the circuit of relationships and believes in connecting through gifts.

Speaking of the genesis of the couple's brain child, Richa talks about the immense support and cooperation she has received from her partner and husband Vipul through this personal and entrepreneurial journey.

"Vipul is the exact opposite of me. So it just feels like we make the best team, working with each other's strengths and weakness, complementing each other," she reveals with a sense of satisfaction.

From negotiating with vendors, to haggling and the tedious task of packaging, the duo has worked in building the startup together from scratch. While Richa remains the primary decision-maker of the business, she stands strong with the unconditional support and insight of her 'partner in crime'. Narrowing down on the range of products was one of the concrete decisions that the two made together. Though spontaneous and quirky in their products, the duo rationalizes in important factors like feasibility and viability of products manufacturing and supply at the scale they are working on at the moment. Once that was finalized, things took a more solid shape for the creative entrepreneur. With perseverance and luck both on her side, Richa received her first corporate order from one of the leading brands in the country. This turn of events not only put Short Circuit on a public platform, but also acted as a great morale booster for the new startup.

"Short Circuit's been like a baby you start living with, and after a point, it becomes everything for you. We're happy to have something like this in our lives. It's lucrative and satisfying and has no hang-ups or cribbing like routine jobs under someone else," she expresses candidly.

In the same spirit of freedom that Short Circuit was started, the forthright experimenter admits to have met no real tough moments in this out of the ordinary climb she has made.

"I think it was only the decision to take the plunge that was challenging. After that, everything has followed naturally."

Speaking of challenges with a stride of strength, she talks about the geographical limitation to Ahmedabad as one hurdle as it slows things down in terms of corporate connections and retail platforms being reachable easily. Having invested her own savings into the business venture, she revels in the financial freedom instead of looking at it as a funding challenge. The spirit and determination with which Richa has taken one bold step after another go on to reveal her strong passion and commitment for Short Circuit. Being a believer in actions speaking more than words, she admits that while reaching out and building contacts with potential clients has not been her strength, the dedication, quality and uniqueness of the brand has spoken for self-publicity. Not having worked on any focused marketing strategy, one might feel that this might affect the popularity and business growth of the enterprise.

"On the contrary, we are able to put all the capital into quality, the product and our employees. We build happy, loyal customers – they are our most effective advertising," she talks about the strategy of Short Circuit as having brought in no investors. We keep on rotating our capital instead of pumping in more money from outside. This is a slow but steady process and will take us a long way," she explains with certainty. Furthering her plans in the near future, Richa also talks about her diversion plans into the sectors of IT and pharmacy. With promising growth and acceptability towards creative products, both sectors have shown significant potential for business and popularity for Short Circuit. Customization and personalization being the key forte of the creative brand, it looks very likely that they will soon be able to acquire clientele amidst the giants.

Looking back at the milestones that have marked the consistent progress of her start up, Richa recollects the first achievement that came in the form of a contract from one of the most prestigious corporations in the country, to design their unique category awards. Just within two months into business and bagging such an important feather in their cap, the team of Short Circuit found themselves exposed to a platform that was being recognized and appreciated by many. It also felt encouraged and motivated them for the forthcoming climb that would only take them higher. Despite being limited by the location of their city, the quirky brand has been able to acquire and retain brands from across the country in different sectors. Supporting this consistent expansion, Short Circuit has also evolved from being a small initiative to being a family of dedicated employees.

"We initially started hiring people once we started expanding, but later realized a more efficient way of working as a startup was by incentivizing our existing employees. This has turned out extremely efficient and effective and we are currently functional with two core members and ten associates in the gang. Crediting a significant support to her friend Vikas and husband Vipul, she explains how a perfect balance between creative freedom and organized strategy has brought Zen between the couple. Having experience in the enterprising industry himself, Vipul has contributed and mentored Richa through the nuances of creating her own enterprise. Speaking not only about people at the professional front, the couple also acknowledges the love and support they have received from their families. While Richa gets her entrepreneurial streak from her father, who is a businessman himself, she goes on to express her gratitude to her parents-in-law, who have not only strengthened her ambitions, but also provided help and unconditional support, making it easier for the businesswoman to achieve her work-home balance.

The balance that the couple maintains at work is only a continuation of their harmony in their personal life. Despite being completely opposite of each other, they form the perfect balance of creativity and logic, freedom and organization, spontaneity and planning.

"I think the key to being a happy couple is to continue being your own individual, unique self. It's the difference that makes the strongest harmony," she adds, clearly from personal experience. Keeping their equation very practical and symbiotic, Vipul and Richa follow the 'act first' policy in major decision making and believe that whoever takes the first concrete action gets the say in cases of mutual disagreements. While this simple point of view gives them both the liberty to keep themselves open to acting according to their opinions, it also allows for mutual respect and acceptability, a key ingredient for making relationships work, both at the personal and professional levels. The ethos is reflected in both their lives as well as their enterprise – of appreciating and encouraging the creative independent streak of the brand.

The way forward for Short Circuit is to increase presence and popularity in all the metro cities in the country by the end of this year by stationing themselves in different retail outlets. With this categorical plan in mind, all growth is now being directed for product marketing accordingly. One might wonder if growth comes with threats and competition.

"We are unique in our own way and we are here to make our mark. We will do it in our way, irrespective of what trends are around us, without comparison with anyone else," speaks a content and straightforward Richa.

As people who have broken trends and gone on to make their own statement, Richa and Vipul today stand as an example of faith and inspiration that one can find in their own creativity and calling. As a couple, as well as individuals, they stand as a symbol of productive harmony and individuality all at once. They even go on to burst the myth about couples in real life not making the best partners in business. If one is looking for a quirky, creative and out of the box example to see and learn from, the couple is their answer!

For customized and ready to use quirky gifts with a pinch of spice and fun, visit www.shortcircuit.in or follow them on Facebook at /shortcircuit.in.

Established by **Amit & Natasha** *with the motive of providing funds for the betterment of stray animals across the city,* **Soulflower** *has now become a leading brand of natural aroma products and a pioneer of the unique concept of providing spa at home.*

An Aromatic Experience – SOULFLOWER

By Amit & Natasha

Amit dropped out of his engineering course from MIT to pursue something more than just education. At the tender age of fourteen, Amit had already exhibited his keen interest for entrepreneurship and had earned an opportunity of being influenced directly by some of the stalwarts in the business world like Sanjay Lalbhai, and Venugopal Dhoot. With such strong conviction and great mentorship, there was no doubt in the fact that Amit was instinctively an entrepreneur. Natasha, on the other hand, pursued her degree in architecture from one of the most popular schools of the country. While exploring different interests, they met on an online portal and got talking. As they got to know each other, they realized that there was an instant chemistry between the two of them.

The only natural thing to happen then was for them to get together, get into a relationship that would eventually lead to marriage. But where the story ends for most people after marriage, for this unique couple, things began to take a more interesting and challenging turn. Amit had already been pursuing his entrepreneurial goals with many years of experience and skills and wanted to start something new which would be both innovative and challenging, with an aim to put his enterprising spirit to its optimum drive. Natasha, during her pursuit of her calling for creativity had grown to realize that she wanted to do more than just conventional architecture and was looking forward to creating an opportunity to explore something in design. Her intimacy with nature is also one of the reasons why she wanted to step out of traditional jobs of architecture and find new dreams around nature. With the determination of the dynamic duo, explorations led to discoveries and an opportunity was sighted in the dimension of healthcare. However, typical to the style and taste of Amit and Natasha, their perspective towards this sector was unique, challenging and path breaking.

"In the recent past, there has been an upward curve observed amongst people who have started showing interest towards healthcare. Which means, people are now more concerned about their appearance as a whole. Here, lack of time plays an important factor. Pampering oneself requires time. That's when we thought of providing easy to use solutions which were natural as well," Sameer reflects behind the rationale of picking up this course of action towards their enterprise. Thus, after incubation and diligent planning, was born a joint venture of Amit and Natasha by the name Soulflower.

The main objective behind the creation of this venture was to generate funds to cater for the stray animals across the city. Amazing, right?! This action tells you what big animal lovers they are! They also know the importance of time, and that going to a spa to pamper oneself is very time consuming. Hence they came up with this idea of 'spa@home' where people can pamper themselves at home, even with very little time.

Elaborating on what their brain child is at its core, Natasha explains how Soulflower focusses on providing a phenomenal experience to its users. Making it more than just a healthcare range, she explains that it's about an elevated lifestyle.

"Combining beauty and fun, we are India's leading brand of natural aroma products and pioneer of the unique concept of providing spa services at home, which has become a revolution today," she shares with pride.

Throwing light on the brand and its identity, Amit explains the uniqueness of Soulflower as the attraction for the customers. If something touches the soul and helps it blossom naturally like a flower, one is happy. It is the essence of what Soulflower offers. While reflecting strongly on its premium appeal, the brand offers a serene, ethereal and natural solution to the healthy well-being of people. More than being a product offered to customers, this unique service is also a reflection of the passion and vision of the couple who believe in an elevated perspective towards life.

Unlike most traditional entrepreneurs who shy away from partnering with their life partners, Amit firmly believes that choosing Natasha as his business partner has been the most rational and fruitful decision. Not only does the duo connect over a multitude of interests, they also bring their own diverse set of skills and experiences to the table, thus contributing to a more holistic development of Soulflower.

"Natasha has a very good eye for detail and adds tremendous value to the branding and creative side of the enterprise. It made perfect sense to have somebody on board who has so much talent and can bring a unique light to the business. Why would I go to an outsider if I can find someone who is so trustworthy right here?" Amit speaks with absolute faith.

Being able to contribute to different fields of action, Amit and Natasha have been able to monitor and evolve multiple dimensions of the business, instead of concentrating on one end of the string.

Not only has this helped them grow faster, but also saved them the trouble of chances of deceit or dead ends that dependence on outsiders might have led to.

Like any other entrepreneur, they too faced many failures. But they never gave up.

"Everyone faces failure at some point in their lives, but the key here is to keep trying, rectifying your mistakes and doing it right. You will definitely find success," speaks a confident Amit.

They believe in their customers, and any advice from them is valuable. According to them, to solve any problem with the right solution, customers are the best advisors; they know exactly where, what went wrong. They take customer amenities very seriously; they want them to be happy and satisfied with the products they provide.

As a niche product catering to the personal needs of people today, Soulflower has already managed to establish its loyal chain of customers. As one of India's leading brand of aromatherapy products, the venture caters to the most definitive need of the population of the urban India. Hitting the bull's eye, the strategic marketing and product designing of the brand has been able to make room in the hearts of its customers by providing them a pampered and soothing experience that not only creates a memorable experience, but also contributes to loyal following and brand endorsement by word of mouth. As a perfect blend of business management with creative expression, the partnership of the entrepreneur and the designer has turned out to create an exemplary model of symbiosis. With the husband-wife duo standing up blindly for each other, even the most testing times get simplified.

Having your life partner as your work partner can make things easy, but that doesn't change the fact that starting an enterprise can be a different battle in itself. Finding funding for an off-beat idea did not come easy. Eventually, they had to bootstrap and invest from their own savings in order to get the business up and running. Although this daring decision put them up on their feet and enabled them to take the initial steps, it still came at a cost. Not being in the position to spend lavishly, they were deprived from the luxury of making a lot of investments in PR or marketing that would otherwise have escalated their popularity and reach from the time of initiation. Instead, they counted heavily on the word of mouth by clients based on the experience of Soulflower's products. However, despite the cringe of capital, the combination of Amit and Natasha's exemplary talent got them to sail through the tough times, and eventually surface as a leading brand. With the advantage of having Natasha by his side, Amit found unconditional support. Coming from an equation built on understanding and respect for each other, it helped them to take difficult decisions.

"Just the sheer relief of not having the fear of being cheated was a big boost. I have seen so many businesses going down the drain because either the partners deceived each other or bailed out during crucial situations. I have to say, I am lucky to have a partner I can blindly trust," Amit confesses with a smile.

Despite the hurdles and deficiency of resources, Soulflower has reached its current state of achievement. Moreover, the commitment, and the compatibility of the duo has a lot to do with that. One of the biggest moments of success was when the venture went online, thereby increasing its reach and scale by multiple times. From a stage where even funding was a crisis, to having reached a thousand towns each month, they clearly have come a long way. Not only does Natasha acknowledge Amit's dedicated passion into making the business rise to an appreciable height, but she also humbly admits to have found a dream that twirls her interests into reality. The gratitude that the two feel for each other reflects strongly in their attitude not only towards each other, but also towards their work. Working with a team of a hundred people who have excitedly come on-board with Soulflower, they humbly acknowledge the contributions that everyone has made with their hard work to evolve the enterprise. Just like Amit's own journey of learning how to become an entrepreneur, he believes in imparting the same to his team.

"I look for passion and excitement in my employees. I believe that knowledge is formed on the way, along with the experiences, hence I stress on creating a learning experience for everyone here at Soulflower," Amit glows with his energy as he talks about his brain child, clearly radiating the sentiments of how much it means to him.

With the entire organization working as a large organism, the couple believes in clearly defining roles not only for everyone in the team, but also for each other, with a clear intention of keeping each other involved and informed about the flow of events and developments.

"Amit is the customer custodian with insights, marketing and sales, and finance as part of his role, while I take care of design, SCM, production and creatives. While we may seem like two tangents in the business, it keeps us both deeply connected with each other and the experience in one segment definitely helps to strengthen the other," Natasha shares her insight.

With eyes wide open towards their plans of expansion in the future, that couple has been categorically working towards intensifying their reach in the country. Although as a brand for wellness and health, Soulflower does consider a few other brands as its competitors, but the dynamic duo believes that their uniqueness and passion for achieving the best and maintaining a continuum of evolution is what will keep them on the edge of success – truly an exciting way to run an enterprise!

Behind the glorious banner of health and experiential well-being, one wonders what it takes to keep the couple going in this together, and whether this picture perfect equation is too good to be true.

"There are conflicts, no doubt; we both have a lot of independent ideas and philosophies that may or may not synchronize with each other. But that does not stop us from expressing our views rationally," speaks a candid Amit. The couple acknowledges that the differences do sometimes transcend the boundaries of work and reach home into their personal space. However, with maturity and understanding, they look at the bigger picture and entertain such differences with the sole motive of helping each other grow, both professionally and personally. Having seen each other through the thick and thin, it is safe to say that Amit and Natasha have reached a stage of holding an equation that transcends egos, personal motives or qualms. "With about fifteen years of working together for Soulflower, there really are no more boundaries of what is personal and what is professional for us. We are lucky enough to have found a career in something that is so personal for us, and luckier to have each other to make this experience a delightful one!" Amit exclaims.

Having celebrated all big and small achievements together, the couple looks back at the times when starting Soulflower from scratch brought them even closer to each other.

"The time when Amit and I made our first soap together will always be a memorable one for me. Soulflower has been our little baby and made us stronger as a family," Natasha speaks emotionally.

"Soulflower is growing rapidly; its aroma has to spread in every home. It won't stop here; it will go on for generations. We will innovate and evolve ourselves, making sure we are present in everyone's heart." Amit mentions sharing his memories. "Each day at Soulflower is memorable. But to see the happy expressions on our consumers' faces is the best. I still remember the response of our first consumer – it makes me so happy."

After that feedback, they have grown, and have never stopped.

As an ideal example for aspiring entrepreneurs to observe and follow, Amit and Natasha have shown unconditional faith, not just in their own talent and conviction, but also in each other. That has been the key to their sustained track of success. As a genuine well-wisher for aspiring entrepreneurs, Amit holds a soft corner for eager learners, and rightfully endorses the idea of partnering up with their life-partners as a blessing. Advising them with his words of wisdom, he adds, "Have confidence in each other's ability, define roles, revenue sharing, and deliverables, and yes, always have the courage to discuss anything across the table."

Summing up everything that has worked in favor of Soulflower and the beautiful couple, one can surely access the mantra to the well-being of a business that flourishes on the spine of a trusting and compatible partnership.

SOULFLOWER For quality aroma experience and a wide range of products that give you the pleasures of a spa at home, visit www.soulflower.biz or follow them on Facebook at /besoulflowerindia.

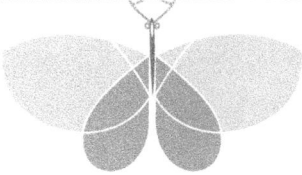

WEARMATES

XB WedMEGood

"As a power couple, both individuals bring to the table something extraordinary. They learn from each other, support one another and succeed together."

Radhika & Abhinav *had stayed away from home long enough to be craving for authentic regional food, especially sweets.* **Sweets InBox** *was started up to provide the authentic food experience to people across India, with just a click of the mouse, with the sweets delivered to your doorstep.*

A Sweet Love Story! – SWEETS INBOX

By Radhika & Abhinav

It is a very well-known fact that the way to a man's heart is through his stomach. Everything is done in this busy life so that one is able to enjoy a happy, hearty meal, which is a true symbol of contentment. However, it happens so often that what one loves to eat is either not accessible or not available at that point. And the heart is left wanting, especially when it comes to the matter of sweets! Every Indian heart understands the craving for sweets – sweets that they may have tasted at some point of time either while growing up in their hometowns, or while travelling to other places where they may have encountered the sheer bliss of a colloquial dessert. However, their daily routine leaves them with only lingering memories of that flavour. What if there was a solution for such craving hearts which wouldn't need to travel half way across the country to find that same fresh and pure flavour? Somewhere in the bustling city of Pune, a couple, with their hearts yearning for traditional sweets from all across the country, took it up as their mission to turn things around. Understanding the craving that people with a sweet tooth like them suffer everywhere, they decided to make a living out of it in their own innovative manner.

This story could have ended very differently with the duo probably carrying on with their lives and marrying very different people, because the first time, Radhika had rejected the proposal to meet Abhinav in the traditional Indian way of an arranged marriage.

"My parents insisted, so Abhinav and I met to see whether we were at all compatible with each other," recalls Radhika with a sense of irony.

It was at their first meeting that the two realized they had a lot of interests in common. Without even realizing it, they connected on common interests like travelling, trying out different cuisines from across the country and an unlikely interest in interior decoration. What had been predicted as an obligatory meeting out of family compulsions ended up with engaging conversations and an instant click between the two. This triggered an interest in their hearts for each other and eventually led to many more meetings. As fate would have it for Radhika and Abhinav, this interest developed into courtship that lasted for almost a year after which they got married in December, 2011.

Before they got married, the two had been leading very independent and successful lives on their own. An engineer by profession with a Master's degree in finance, Abhinav has over eight years of experience in the IT industry and has been working as a senior consultant. Radhika is an architect by mainstream definitions of a profession and her interests lie deeply in exploring different kinds of cuisines with local flavours all over the country. Clearly, the two had been doing well in their careers and marriage should have brought no significant change. But sometimes it takes the right person to come into your life to show you unexplored paths. Abhinav had been gradually growing tired of his routine work, although it was extremely lucrative and got him to travel to many places. Despite all this, it did not offer the challenge and excitement that he wanted to experience. Radhika, on the other hand, had been contemplating to start something of her own and become a freelancer. With support from each other, the two explicitly penned down their ambitions and set together on a path that combined both their passion and interests in life. While both have been living in Pune for quite some time, Abhinav hails from Rajasthan, and Radhika from Chattisgarh. And being foodies, they missed their local sweets.

"We always noticed how dependent you have to be on people coming from home to bring back sweets because you particularly missed that flavour and essence. Also, Radhika incidentally has a traditional sweet shop run by the family back home in Chattisgarh," Abhinav speaks about the genesis of their business idea. Taking insight from a traditional sweet shop that gets calls for orders from across the country, the two decided to tap on this market gap. With an aim to provide sweets that are fresh and pure to people across India, a venture was created by the two with the name of Sweets InBox. Starting to engage customers through the online portal, Sweets InBox has been set up as a platform utilizing the rising e-commerce vogue in the country.

After the duo quit their stable and lucrative jobs, it was important to have a strong foothold for the startup. Since the two had no prior experience in entrepreneurship, materializing things from ground zero was a big challenge for them. Radhika recollects with a tense expression about the time when quitting their jobs and starting something so uncertain seemed to be wrought with trouble.

"Our parents were visibly unhappy with this decision. In fact, we haven't really been able to win their full-fledged support even now."

However, there was more to the incoming challenges once the venture was launched in 2014 than just family affairs.

"Procuring funds was not easy, but we did manage to find some angel funding by people who had belief and an understanding of our concept and passion," Abhinav speaks in retrospection. As a venture just starting out, establishing a trustable network with vendors was no easy task. Not only was it difficult to connect with sweet makers from all over the country, but even with those they connected, such a concept was very alien to both the vendors and the clients. Hence establishing a smooth function from order to delivery was extremely challenging.

"There were times when the vendor failed to deliver on time, or the product delivered was not up to the mark. There was the challenge of insuring that service was meeting the quality that the brand was claiming to make," he explains.

While the duo has expertise in creative design, marketing, and finance, smoothening operations was something that took a while for them to understand and master. However, there was constant support from friends, relatives and food bloggers from different parts of the country, who extended a helping hand. For a startup dedicated in an unconventional vertical, it hasn't been easy to bring people on board.

"We have a lot of trouble hiring people. Although people have started getting attracted towards startups now, but since we're fairly new and not into a segment like lifestyle or fashion where a lot of brands have already established themselves, it's difficult to win people's confidence," Radhika speaks with experience.

Since the couple was boot-strapping with only the most basic funds available, there was no luxury of spending on marketing and brand building. However, despite the challenges, the dedicated duo has brought out their passion in building Sweets InBox into an appreciable stature.

With a service that is committed to ensuring that fresh and pure sweets are delivered at the doorstep, Sweets InBox is a true symbol of the passion that Abhinav and Radhika share for their interest. To prepare and motivate themselves for this enterprise, the couple had spent over six months in research and market assessment to understand what they were getting into. Abhinav, who holds great interest in e-commerce, has always been attracted to this dimension. As it turns out, the easiest and most economical method to reach a large scale and geography of customers is through online platforms, hence it was the most natural course of action for the duo.

"The term 'sweets' has a universal and simplistic appeal; it's easy to remember and search online, and 'inbox' is just what we are offering; your favorite sweets are delivered beautifully in a box, and can be accessed through a simple click online, hence 'inbox' sounded like an appropriate suffix," explains the creative Radhika who is responsible for product designing and building the brand value. Between the two of them, work and responsibilities are skillfully split to the best of their abilities and interests. While Radhika brings creativity, design, marketing strategies and product designing on the table, Abhinav brings forth his IT and finance experience to contribute to the brand. Although a missing element between the two of them was operations, but always eager to learn, Abhinav took on a supporting academic course from one of the most premier institutes of the country and acquired in-depth mentorship from some of the stalwarts on entrepreneurship to gain insight and knowledge with great attention to details about starting an enterprise. Hence, with time and experience, the confidence has built up to take things forward despite all the challenges. With compatibility and support from each other, the duo has evolved their personal skills as well as the enterprise from ground zero to being acknowledged amidst the top ten couple entrepreneurs by *The Economic Times*. During this journey, there have been several occasions for learning and growing for the two who have taken well to such forward steps.

"We have had several occasions when people have liked our product and service so much that they have come back for more. There have also been times when we've lost big contracts because of a problem with a link in the chain, causing us losses. But in either case, we get to learn a lot. The joy of receiving a thank you call, or someone's feedback about how we have brought back old memories associated with the local sweets, is just priceless!" Abhinav speaks ecstatically about the journey of Sweets InBox.

Starting from nothing, they have grown to a team of seven dedicated members who help them from back end to quality assurance. Between the two of them, Abhinav and Radhika have shared responsibilities at the work front with mutual understanding between them. While Abhinav heartily declares his wife to be the main decision maker of both business and home, Radhika gives the entire credit for this initiative to her husband who has been responsible for conceptualizing Sweets InBox while her contributions for relationship building and negotiations have helped for the venture to come this far within an year of operations. Still not recognizing their accomplishment as a mark of success, the ambitious couple has set a goal to acquiring ten thousand and more customers and becoming a common household name. While their expansion has been aggressive and steady, there have been plenty of competitors from the more established brands of sweets that are expanding to the online mode. However, never shying away from competition, the duo loves staying on their toes with constant efforts towards improvement.

Speaking of partnerships, one might wonder what it's like to have a business partner who is also your partner in life. However, breaking stereotypes and inhibitions, the duo has set an example of such selfless understanding of each other that it becomes a life worth learning from.

"We share our work and concerns with each other with utmost honesty. I think that's why we understand each other so well," Radhika adds about her equation with Abhinav. "But we ensure that work does not spill over into our personal space where we try to spend time with each other so that we grow as individuals and as a family with our two-year-old kid."

Sharing a partnership with someone you know so well comes with its share of comfort, Abhinav explains, as there is utmost trust and compatibility where you don't have to spend an extra share of your attention as you would have to if you had an outsider as a business partner. Sharing each experience and achievement has new meaning altogether for this couple as they have worked on things from scratch and seen each other through thick and thin.

"It's easy to keep things going when times are easy, but you get to see real strength in a relationship when times are tough. We have been very lucky to have each other's support through our times of trial, and that has brought us closer," Radhika reveals with a smile of contentment on her face. Each one has also gone out of the way to share interests and hobbies of the other. While Radhika has revealed her faith in Abhinav by jumping in with full faith into his idea of the enterprise, Abhinav too makes unconditional efforts to understand her passion, to the extent of taking up a short course of interior designing to be able to connect with the ideas of his wife.

While striving to turn their craving into a full-fledged entrepreneurial affair, the duo has sent out a much deeper message of happiness. Whether it is the tearful smile of the old couple that finds a modak delivered to their door step, or an excited sister being able to reach to her brother outside the country, the spirit of passion and joy existing in the lives of Abhinav and Radhika radiates, inspiring many others who dream of not only breaking away from their monotonous lives to follow their passion, but also of path breaking efforts made to carve their own niche in today's world. While the two have sweet nothings to share with each other, they are sharing a plenty of sweets with the rest of the country!

To satisfy your taste buds or to give someone living away from home a wonderfully sweet surprise, visit www.sweetsinbox.com, or their Facebook page on / sweetsinbox/.

Breaking the myth that personal relations cannot mature into a professional partnership, these SuperCouples have set a new trend and carved a niche for their work in the mainstream markets and their consumers' hearts.

Udai & Shruti *come from varied educational fields, but their love for each other and the love for art made them start up* **Wearmates**. *It offers a wide range of creative wearable products, with the right amount of style, spunk and depth.*

A Creative Compliment! – WEARMATES

By Udai & Shruti

In a small room in Delhi, a bunch of artists talk, scribble, draw and talk some more. With pens and colours, on papers and on clothes, art is oozing out of every inch of this room. There is music playing in sync with the general mood and creativity is meeting new boundaries of expression. A few years, some rooms and several platforms later, this is still what every day is like for some people. Finding meaning in creativity and creativity in expression is more than passing time or even a profession for some people. For the likes of creative butterflies, such is the way of life. And such souls are found in the most everyday looking people like our classmates, colleagues, neighbours or people you walk past on a busy traffic street. It takes a little more looking to find out what's below the surface of the ordinary to find excellence that is making wonders around us. When people with such passions surface into the mainstream, they change definitions of trends, break boundaries of what is accepted as common. Such is the life story of Shruti and Udai, who have made a new convention of what art is, as also consumable art products.

A resident of Delhi, Udai is an engineer and holds a Master's degree in international business. Shruti is from Patna and has an equally diverse educational background with a Bachelor's degree in political science and degrees in international business and public relations. An artist at heart, she had begun her first creative expression when she started painting for her brother funky t-shirts to wear during his graduation years. Not only did she find herself being extremely fond of what she was doing, but also came to realize that his brother and a lot of his friends seemed to love her designs. As destiny had schemed, she crossed paths with Udai at his birthday party where they were introduced by Udai's best friend. What could have been any other encounter turned into a connection of magic, where art, love and life transcended between the two souls and hence began the story of Shruti and Udai. As a close friend fondly says about them, "Shruti painted for the love of art, and Udai painted for the love of Shruti."

But what began with innocent liking and interest soon developed into a more serious commitment and partnership in ways that predictable relationships do not usually mature. While carrying on with their seemingly conventional lives of stable jobs, a stable relationship and their respective spaces in general, the two were also harnessing their dream for a more out of the box future. With a set of friends and artists, several sessions of ideation and brain storming were held in Delhi. Thoughts were proposed and rejected, ideas tried and tested; art styles experimented and improved. The aim was to create something unique and expressive that would break stereotyes. After one-and-a-half years of this persistence, the team members quit their stable and lucrative jobs in big corporates to come together to form Wearmates, with an aim to follow a more challenging, daring and expressive expression through entrepreneurship in times when startups were still struggling to be taken seriously in the Indian mainstream business. That's how the creative and entrepreneurial journey of Shruti and Udai began in 2013.

"Our vision was simple. We wanted to produce unique products in a way to make art available in the most wearable forms", Shruti explains. "Of course it was the getting there part that was a lot more than simple," she adds jokingly. What had started as a fun-filled activity for the artist as painting T-shirts took a more organized and commercial angle as things moved ahead.

"Before starting Wearmates, we had been painting a lot for friends and friends of friends on t-shirts, kurtas, caps and much more; they loved our work!" Udai explains about the advent of the enterprising journey. Once the decision to make their idea go live had been made, the real climb uphill began. The struggle of narrowing down on the products out of the entire range of possibilities was not an easy feat for the expressionists to begin with. Keeping in mind the trends of artistic wearables and the niche they wanted to create, team Wearmates focused on catering to unique designs for trendy wearables in a way which is both artful and attractive. The name Wearmates, stands as a perfect expression of creating wearable products that express a bond between the creatives and the consumers. With the same swankiness that the brand represents, its products have just the right amount of spunk, style and depth.

What may seem like a picture perfect scenario has actually taken to shape through a lot of hard work and struggle for the couple.

"Leaving our lucrative jobs for something so unpredictable wasn't an easy decision to make. When you are an entrepreneur, you are responsible for every single decision being made in the organization, even the one that you are making out of assumptions or future projections. This can be scary at times," Udai expresses with sincerity.

Functioning out of their saving reserves, the couple had to work with a shoe-string budget in the initial days. A lot of friends and family came together to support them in kick-start funding. Shruti's brother, who is very close to the couple, was a strong pillar of support – financial, emotional and experiential for the then starting out entrepreneurs. However, without the luxury of external funding, the effort was a grilling one and there were limitations. Even as the couple gallantly overcame the financial challenge with wise and gradual investment into Wearmates, the brand still had to go through the struggles of breaking the clutter of the so-called artistic brands that had already established a strong market name and value. Having decided to use the online marketing channel for their marketing and purchase, Wearmates was ready with its own website and virtual exhibitions of products, only to realize that to acquire and retain traffic on the website would not be easy for a new brand that has not been heard of. All these challenges kept the duo on their toes for a while as they worked consistently on strengthening and expanding their model.

With will and perseverance come wonderful results, and Shruti and Udai have plentiful of those. Linking Wearmates to popular e-commerce websites not only started getting them visibility and acknowledgement, but also resulted in increasing traffic and successful conversion of purchase on their own website!

"We introduced t-shirts at the start, and they are still one of our primary products. We introduced a plethora of different products – bags, totes, canvas shoes and wallets. Experimentation helped us to know the market better, because there is a fine line between what you are selling and what the customer wants. We gauged it at an early level and learnt the most important lesson that customer is the king," Shruti answers about the initial approach and strategy. Turning their challenges into their strengths, the couple thoughtfully started developing their online visibility in a way that was unique, catchy and catered exactly to the needs of their target audience. The two have come together with an effective blend of expression and experience along with their insight to excel in this arena.

"We are doing what we do best – to create, to express and to make it stand out from the rest. I guess when something comes so deeply and naturally for you, it's difficult to go wrong," Udai speaks for the both of them.

Talking categorically about future plans, Udai explains their expansion plans, "We have grown internally from the time of our inception. We plan to enter retail sales through showrooms, have a wedding collection to storm the Indian markets, partner with more companies to increase visibility and of course look out for newer channels for exports."

Working in an environment of constant growth and development, the couple looks at evolving competition as a great opportunity to keep them on their toes and aspiring for better and more creative explorations. "We know we are competing for excellence. If it comes in the form of other brands, we welcome that too, as it is only going to inspire us to grow and evolve in the long run," Shruti adds with a remarkable sense of insight and maturity.

Speaking of their continually evolving spirit and style, Shruti has this to say about the drive that gets them going, "It's always about doing better and pushing our creative boundaries and seeing what new can come out of the ideas."

For the last six months, the brand has been experimenting and expressing with designs for their female footwear section. The uniqueness of their focus and style of work is more than a reflection of how extraordinary their ideas are. What makes it even more heart-warming is that such creative outflow does not remain confined to ideas, but finds form in actual products that are loved and appreciated by their constantly increasing fan following.

'You are the best, you got a smile on my dad's face.' This is what a particular customer who got an image for her dad made on a t-shirt had to say.

"We made her a caricature of her dad on a t-shirt, and she came back to us, only this time with her dad wearing the same t-shirt!" Udai's excitement and contentment go on to reveal a lot about the accomplishment that he feels today after having joined his soulmate in her passion. It is only natural that their partnership for life has been achieving new levels of success with each endeavor.

"We have been featured in several magazines and newspapers. We even featured in the online website YourStory. When your passion and dedication starts earning such recognition, it feels great and works as an amazing morale booster for us and the team," explains a humble Shruti.

With an environment that nurtures creativity and expression, Wearmates is a perfect workplace for art oriented people. The current team comprises the verticals of management, craftsmen and artisans making a total of nine members. Udai takes care of operations and craftsmanship while Shruti nurtures design and art. With a perfect amalgamation of their skills in their respective areas of expertise, the duo maintains a perfect balance between individuality and team work. Being involved and encouraging, they respect the steps taken by their counterpart with full faith and confidence.

"We are looking out for each other with trust and commitment. That's what keeps us steady and stable."

Shruti talks about the mantra that has brought the couple to break the myths of couples not making the best of business partners. She speaks for the both of them when she generously appreciates the bond they have achieved. The couple tied the nuptial knot in 2016 and believe that they have a matured and mutual admiration for each other. With their passions and commitments aligned, they deal with disagreements as an opportunity to evolve, as they do for their successes.

"If one stumbles, the other one gives support; when one is leading, the other encourages. That is how a healthy partnership works," Udai talks about seeing many rising entrepreneurs who are partners in their personal life too and sends a word of encouragement to them.

As partners for life, as well as individuals who have broken creative and conventional boundaries, Shruti and Udai stand today as an example of the spirit of dreaming big and working passionately to actualize those dreams. Working with your soulmate can have many different dimensions to it, but the way this couple has celebrated and accentuated each other's persona and experiences is hard to find.

"It's a universal fact, no two minds think alike. Being a spouse doesn't guarantee that you will agree upon every decision taken. We do have differences of opinion regarding our work styles. It's best to talk things out and that's what we've maintained. A work-life balance is very essential to maintain." Shruti sums up the very essence of finding the right way of partnership.

Inspiring many others with their creative and extraordinary journey, both as life partners as well as entrepreneurs, theirs is a story that reveals a lot about the potential that is building in today's scenario which is open to experimentation, exploration and expression, much like the brand Wearmates.

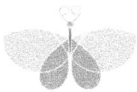

WEARMATES

To stand out of the crowd with funky and customized wearables, visit www.wearmates.com, or follow them on Facebook at /wearmatesclothing.

Mehak & Anand *have set out to simplify gearing up for the most important event of one's life – their wedding.* **Wedmegood** *lists down service providers and furnishes information on exclusive planning and event management of big, fat Indian weddings that can be cherished without getting into the hassles and worries.*

A Wedding beyond the Marriage – WEDMEGOOD

By Mehak & Anand

The best minds and talent getting together is a combination that often leads to phenomenal development. If this combination brings onboard a diversity that can benefit both sides, it is sure to create long lasting relationships. Whether you call it a stroke of chance, or fall of rational events, the result can be both surprising and inspiring. With creativity meeting new heights of perfection in this country, one is able to see a few startups that have broken conventions of profession and motivated people to quit the stable and predictable path they may have been walking for decades. One such example of an inspiring pursuit of creative endeavours is the story of Anand and Mehak. Their journey of meeting unexpectedly, evolving in their relationships, and taking it beyond just the equation of nuptials is an interesting one.

When Anand was pursuing his Master's degree in business administration from one of the most premier colleges of the country, Mehak was acquiring her own Master's degree in economics from one of the best institutes in India. While in their own parallel universes, busy with the perusal of the field they enjoyed the most, the two were also unknowingly drifting in the larger scheme of things towards each other and what brought them together was also their chase towards excellence in their area of interest.

"We actually met while interning for an organization. We might have drifted away from each other with work and other people, but as it so happened that we ended up sharing the same work desk and system! It is serendipity that got us into each other's proximity," Mehak speaks with a sense of awe. What began as a work compulsion turned into an instant connection between the two that sprouted as a healthy friendship and matured into a lasting relationship. While the two travelled around different locations for their education and work, they sustained a long distance relationship for a prolonged period of four years. With its share of unpredictability and instability, the relationship stood strong and blossomed into a beautiful marriage.

Just as unpredictable as their relationship, their fate of extending their partnership beyond marriage also happened as a matter of chance. Anand, the entrepreneur at heart, would always tell Mehak that he would quit his job one day and start something of his own. The charm of a business opportunity always held his interest. Perhaps that is what ultimately led to a surprising turn of events.

"I am a very risk-aversive person. Every time Anand would talk about entrepreneurship, my heart would skip a nervous beat!" Mehak exclaims.

However, some part of her also always wanted to work on something parallel to her job because her love for exploration made her try out different things with minimum risks. It was with this interest that she had started writing a beauty and fashion blog of her own and within no time earned a lot of popularity and fan following. It was in the course of this experiment that the couple unknowingly conceived an extraordinary idea that would change their future, both personal and professional.

"It was during the time of our wedding preparations that I started writing about the entire process on my blog," she recalls. In the face of putting together a wedding, the duo realized what a challenging experience it can be. As a part of the digital generation, they easily gauged the absence of any online service provider to manage a wedding. While Mehak claims only to have mentioned this in passing to Anand, the entrepreneurial bug in him immediately began scanning this observation as a potential business opportunity.

"Unless you give it your all, there is no point," he frequently observes. His extensive research brought to light that several online portals existed outside of India that not only provided all connection with various vendors for a wedding, but also provided applications that could ease the process of various stages of planning needed in the course of a wedding preparation. An Indian customized service on the internet did not exist at the time. Thus, an experience that led to an observation became a golden opportunity, and hence was born a unique enterprise – Wedmegood.

An online wedding planning portal, Wedmegood is a blessing for every bride and groom as it offers precisely everything from tip to toe, that a couple would need from the planning stage to the implementation of their wedding. Not only are these services extremely accessible and convenient, but also provide a uniqueness of being specifically customized and flexible. Apart from providing implementation support, Wedmegood impresses in its creative and attractive inspiration ideas to make the wedding a unique one, with dedicated advisory support. Just like its features and quality, the name of the enterprise also resonates a unique and fresh spirit, and stands for the young and creative drive of the duo that runs the venture. As two people who complemented each other in all their engagements, it was the natural thing for them to get together and bring their own set of perspectives and skills to run Wedmegood together. While it was understood that Anand would contribute to the business management aspect of the enterprise, Mehak's role was extremely crucial in bringing organic traffic and marketing skills. "Having seen her grow through her blog and its evolution from nothing to its popularity till date, I can't think of a better person who I could have brought on board to become my partner in this endeavour. Moreover, it's not just the skills she brings in, but the trust and understanding we can blindly share with each other that makes this partnership valuable," Anand speaks fondly. Nonetheless, it took the nervous Mehak considerable convincing to set sail with his idea. Being keen to pursue something more stable and predictable, she was slightly less motivated. However, Anand's excitement and sheer faith in her got Mehak to break her walls and join him on the high walk of the enterprise. "At worst, I would probably use a year of my mainstream career, that's all I thought. At best, we could create something fantastic," she adds optimistically.

In a scenario of conventional jobs, where most professionals end up doing things entirely distanced from their education or interests, Anand and Mehak are fortunate enough to be able to contribute and build on their interests and optimize on their educational as well as professional credentials. Anand's role in his previous organizations had been in the sales division. Furthermore, his experience of setting up teams from scratch has come in extremely handy in building the spine of Wedmegood. Also, his education has helped him understand the sales skills and he brings them to adequate use in his role. Mehak, on the other hand, has drawn abundantly from her experience of growth with her blog. Knowing what ticks online and what it takes to get customers to trust the brand has turned out to be extremely productive for her. Apart from that, her experience in data analytics helps her to analyze the traffic, usage, trends and feedback flow that help Wedmegood to continuously evolve.

As a startup that has begun its journey fairly recently, Wedmegood has evolved very rapidly. Having seen its share of challenges, there have been plenty of lessons that have helped the couple grow with their perspective and insight. One of the most expected challenges came in the form of Mehak's parents.

"Hailing from a conventionally professional background, it was extremely difficult for my mother to imagine how we had both consciously decided to quit our jobs. She couldn't sleep for many nights," she recalls. Furthermore, having spent most of their savings during the wedding, the couple also felt a considerable financial cringe during the initiation phase. However, Anand, with his exemplary people's skills managed to impress a lot of well-wishers who came on board with generous investments, sufficient to get the ball rolling. More than the challenges in the initial phase, it was the operational experience that highlighted the challenges. While ensuring quality and timely delivery was a challenge they had previously anticipated, the absence of a tech-specialist as a cofounder posed as a relatively big challenge, especially because their strength was being able to deliver a smooth and effective digital service. However, with time, not only did they learn and evolve their own skill sets, but were able to strengthen their coordination with each other and bring to the table their valued insight. The most significant of such turning points came into the life of the entrepreneurs when they got selected as one of the top five startups in a prestigious contest to avail funding. Even though they did not get direct funding from the event, they did attain a lot of popularity and exposure, got an opportunity to learn and refine their pitch, and subsequently landed up closing a round with some of the biggest stalwarts of the country.

One might wonder what it takes to break the trend and partner up with one's partner, mingling business with personal life. However, for this unique couple, it has been the most natural and a favourable decision. Confidently declaring that she would have worked with Anand even if he hadn't been her spouse, Mehak admits that they make amazing business partners. With a deep level of compatibility and understanding for each other, the co-founders are able to gauge each other's decisions in the bigger picture of the enterprise, even if they may or may not agree at a micro level.

"Despite being two very different people, we have our principles in sync. Besides, the more the differences, the broader the range of perspectives, right?" Anand adds zestfully.

Apart from having each other, the couple has also managed to bring up a strong and competent team of seventeen members who are not only efficient in their skills, but are extremely dedicated and passionate about the enterprise. Anand's reputation as a skilled recruiter and a hustler who gets things done to perfection is largely to be credited for this, and Mehak admires these aspects in her husband, only to draw inspiration from his passion. With such a symbiotic relation based on mutual respect and trust, it comes as no surprise then that the couple is able to sail through mutual differences with relative ease.

With such a high degree of involvement and commitment for their work, it is not hard to decipher that for this couple, the boundaries between home and work have transcended long ago.

"It is impossible not to bring work issues back home. Conflicts also do follow. But with experience, we have come to treat them with unbiased opinions. And we do make specific rules about not bringing up differences or even work in the times that we have set aside from everything else, dedicated only for each other as husband and wife," Anand speaks like someone who has matured both as an entrepreneur as well as a husband.

A fresh perspective, a quality service and a partnership that has transcended through all boundaries of challenges and ego trips, these are the qualities that come to light when one witnesses the story of the two co-founders of Wedmegood. Anand and Mehak have set examples of achievements through learning. Not only have they cashed out on an opportunity that arose from their first-hand experience, but also exhibited exceptional endurance in times that pushed them out of their comfort zones. With utmost respect, mutual understanding and a commitment to achieve and deliver the best, they have managed to sustain an enterprise with an out of the box idea. In the process, they have also brought to life their deepest passions in life. This process has been an ongoing evolution for them, both as individuals as well as a couple, both professionally as well as personally. Maintaining a balance between home and work, individuality and partnership, and powers and responsibilities, both Anand and Mehak have emerged strong as partners, entrepreneurs as well as a couple, setting an example for many.

WedMEGood

For hassle-free management of all events and services that you need for managing a wedding, do visit www.wedmegood.com, or Facebook: /wedmegood.

Upcoming title by the same author

SuperSiblings

In this world where relationships make or break the deal for a lifetime, it is imperative to be able to have equations that are reliable, compatible and accessible. Luckily enough, it doesn't take too much effort to find the right set of people, perhaps because nature has its own way of providing them.

From childhood to adulthood, siblings share a lot. They share their environment, principles and interests, and perhaps they also account for compatibility between them.

Gone are the days when siblings only gave the best 'what car to buy' advice or approved the guy you were dating. Today, brothers and sisters are travelling together, taking up hobbies together, and to add to the latest trend, building enterprises together.

Varying from tech startups to trendy fashion wear, from utility applications to artsy expressions, siblings seem to be partnering up with each other to break away from conventional career choices.

SuperSiblings encapsulates the journeys of siblings who have broken away from conventions and supported each other to startup their dream ventures.